INTERNATIONAL LOVE (AND HATE) FOR
PEREz HILTON

—*Rolling Stone*

"The queen of mean."

"One of the most polarizing media figures since Howard Stern."
—*LA Weekly*

"Like a queer-eyed Incredible Hulk, this raging diva persona...has smashed through the Hollywood elite, muscling his way from bottom-feeding blogger to up-and-coming entertainment-business power player."
—*Wired*

"Hollywood's frothy potty-mouthed little drama queen."
—*New York Press*

—*China Daily*

"The blogger Hollywood loves to hate."
—*Forbes*

"A contro... gossinmonger with a poison pen." ... than
... Musto

"Perez ...
IKEA o...

... e ... ome a
"Love ... k Times
blogg...
enter... s in
hard... nessWeek

"Pe... ...
Hol... Advocate

"T... nPost.com

ALSO BY PEREZ HILTON
with JARED SHAPIRO

Red Carpet Suicide

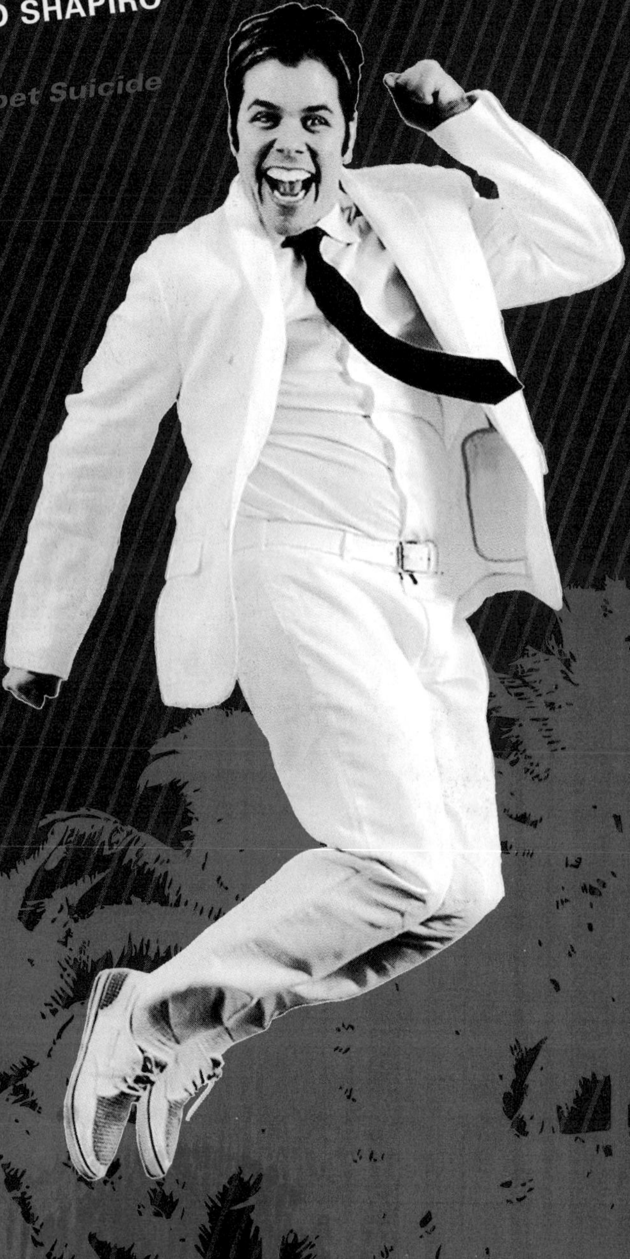

PEREZ HILTON'S
TRUE
BLOGGYWOOD
STORIES

THE GLAMOROUS LIFE OF
BEATING, CHEATING, AND OVERDOSING

PEREZ HILTON
with JARED SHAPIRO

A CELEBRA BOOK

CELEBRA
Published by New American Library, a division of Penguin Group (USA) Inc.,
375 Hudson Street, New York, New York 10014, USA • Penguin Group (Canada),
90 Eglinton Avenue East, Suite 700, Toronto, Ontario M4P 2Y3, Canada (a division of Pearson
Penguin Canada Inc.) • Penguin Books Ltd., 80 Strand, London WC2R 0RL, England • Penguin
Ireland, 25 St. Stephen's Green, Dublin 2, Ireland (a division of Penguin Books Ltd.) • Penguin
Group (Australia), 250 Camberwell Road, Camberwell, Victoria 3124, Australia (a division of
Pearson Australia Group Pty. Ltd.) • Penguin Books India Pvt. Ltd., 11 Community Centre,
Panchsheel Park, New Delhi - 110 017, India • Penguin Group (NZ), 67 Apollo Drive, Rosedale,
North Shore 0632, New Zealand (a division of Pearson New Zealand Ltd.) • Penguin Books
(South Africa) (Pty.) Ltd., 24 Sturdee Avenue, Rosebank, Johannesburg 2196, South Africa

Penguin Books Ltd., Registered Offices:
80 Strand, London WC2R 0RL, England

First published by Celebra,
a division of Penguin Group (USA) Inc.

First Printing, December 2009
10 9 8 7 6 5 4 3 2 1

Photo on page 86 courtesy of Jeff Kravitz/FilmMagic/Getty Images. Photos on pages 8, 10, 45, 145,
and 159 courtesy of Perez Hilton.

Copyright © Cool Lava Entertainment, Inc., 2009
All rights reserved

CELEBRA and logo are trademarks of Penguin Group (USA) Inc.

LIBRARY OF CONGRESS CATALOGING-IN-PUBLICATION DATA

Hilton, Perez, 1978–
  Perez Hilton's true bloggywood stories: the glamorous life of beating,
cheating, and overdosing/Perez Hilton, with Jared Shapiro.
    p. cm.
  "A Celebra book."
  ISBN 978-0-451-23083-6
  1. Celebrities-Humor. 2. Celebrities-Miscellanea. I. Shapiro, Jared.
  II. Title.
  PN6231.C25H547 2009
  818'.602-dc22   2009037478

Set in Univers
Designed by Pauline Neuwirth, Neuwirth & Associates, Inc.

Printed in the United States of America

I'd like to dedicate this book to God.

CONTENTS

SECTION 1: TRUE BLOGGYWOOD STARS   1

INTRODUCTION: 3
WHERE WE ARE RIGHT NOW

TOP 10 CELEBRITIES OF OUR GENERATION   23
AND HOW THEY STAY RELEVANT

THE ANNUAL PEREZZIES   57
FOR EXCELLENCE IN ABSURDITY

TWILIGHT   87
VAMPIRES THAT DON'T SUCK

SECTION 2: BEHIND THE CURTAIN   95

WHAT THEY SAY VS. WHAT THEY MEAN   97
SMELL THE BULL SHIZ

CELEBRITIES WHO TIP OFF THE PAPARAZZI   119
THIS IS HOW IT'S REEEEALLY DONE!

129 **THE MICHAEL JACKSON CATASTROPHE**
WHAT REALLY HAPPENED

139 **THE NEW SKINNIES**
STILL PIN-THIN IN BLOGGYWOOD

143 **WHEN REALITY BITES**
REALITY TV'S BIGGEST BLOODSUCKERS

153 **BACK BY POPULAR DEMAND**
THE BEST UNCONFIRMED RUMORS I WISH WERE TRUE:
BLOWING THE LID OFF HOW IT'S DONE

163 **SECTION 3: BEYOND THE CURTAIN**

165 **TOP 10 PREDICTIONS**
FOR THE NEXT BIG BLOGGYWOOD DRAMAS COMING
TO A BLOG NEAR YOU SOON

173 **THE FUTURE OF YOUNG HOLLYWOOD**
HOW THEIR LITTLE MONSTERS WILL TURN OUT

181 **SPLIT OR GET MARRIED**
WHO WILL MAKE IT, WHO WON'T, AND WHY

SECTION 4: LIFTING THE CURTAIN   191

JON AND KATE PLUS 8   193
EVERYTHING YOU DIDN'T KNOW YOU WANTED TO
KNOW

THE UNIVERSITY OF PEREZ   197
LECTURES FOR THE BLOGGYWOOD MAJOR

THE QUESTIONS BARBARA WALTERS   209
WOULD NEVER ASK
GETTING DOWN TO THE NITTY-GRITTY

THINGS THAT MAKE YOU GO "WHAT   213
THE FUCK?"
AKA STUFF I FIND REALLY WEIRD ABOUT
HOLLYWOOD

PEREZ ON PEREZ   219
TAKING A PEEK UNDER MY OWN HOOD

STOP THE PRESS!   225

ACKNOWLEDGMENTS   230

1

TRUE BLOGGYWOOD STARS

WHERE WE ARE RIGHT NOW

Howdy, ffff . . . friends! Whoops, almost said the F word again. Yes, I'm back, this time many pounds lighter. Gettin' action, gettin' into trouble, and, as usual, being a busy blogger.

Recently, I launched CocoPerez, my new blog hot spot located at the intersection of Hot Mess Celebrity St. and To-Die-For Fashion Ave. So, that's where I'm at.

But where are all the celebrities at? It's been just about a year since I released *Red Carpet Suicide* and the scandals keep on coming like a bad case of herpes!

For a while it seemed like all was quiet in Hollywood. Jen Aniston was dating her rock star cub, John Mayer, Brad and Angelina weren't fighting (or at least they hid it very well), Jessica Simpson scored an NFL football star for a boyfriend, and Jon and Kate had eight kids. Ho-hum, right? Until Nadya Suleman, who already had six kids, then gave birth to seven—no, wait! There's an eighth hiding in there!—and all of a sudden she was a "mom" to fourteen kids. Hollywood, like Octomom, at any given moment can just suddenly pop out a giant sack of new BBs screaming for attention.

Hollywood, like Octomom, at any given moment can just suddenly pop out a giant sack of new BBs screaming for attention.

And like K-Fed's baby-making stick, Tinseltown hardly ever manages to keep anything under wraps. So why did Jen get dumped not once, not twice, but three times in a row? Why did Octomom become so famous? Was Michael Jackson murdered or did he die a slow death at the hands of MANY killers?

Well, I'm here to get to the bottom of all that. In the fast-and-loose world I call PEREZ HILTON'S TRUE BLOGGYWOOD

STORIES, we get to lift the veil of celebrity and peek at what's really under there. On the blinding surface of celebrity glamour, we see their riches, their train of sexy costars, and the lives we dream of having. But it's interesting to see the underside of celebrities exposed, you know. Celebrities seem to live in a bubble of managers, publicists, lawyers, waitresses, producers, assistants, and fans who will do ANYTHING they ask them to do. When we see what their private lives are really like, we realize all the expensive hair weaves in El Lay can't keep a star immune from heartbreak. It was almost touching to watch Britney Spears open the doors to her small world of handlers on MTV and find out how sheltered, self-absorbed, and naive she really is. When the veil of fame is lifted, the real celebrity is exposed. And that's what we'll find in Bloggywood—the conspiracy theories, the speculations, the innuendos, the glimmering illusion versus the grainy videos shown on the gazillions of copycat sites out there. In short, all the tawdry scandals that kept us coming back to Bloggywood for more.

Anyways, speaking of bad cases of herpes, it seems like 2009's scandals weren't all necessarily Paris Hilton- and Lindsay Lohan-based for once. We traded drugs and DUIs for divorces, newborns, and mysterious deaths. But it wasn't the A-list this year that did it to us. In fact, a whole new group of celebrities emerged. "Faux-leb-rities," let's call them.

Speaking of bad cases of herpes, it seems like 2009's scandals weren't all necessarily Paris Hilton- and Lindsay Lohan-based for once.

A "Faux-lebrity" is someone who for one reason or another just ended up being famous. Accidentally on purpose, of course. It used to be you had to be supernaturally gorgeous, infinitely wealthy, hung like a bull, ripped from head to toe, the child of famous parents, or—and here's the shocker—talented. Then, all of a sudden, people started getting famous for other reasons, like big balls (Cisco Adler), giving birth as a man (Thomas Beattie), or horrible renditions of Whitney Houston classics (thank you, *American Idol* rejects).

But big balls and transgender pregnancies aren't the onlyyyy way to become famous. In fact, as of recent, you don't have to have any physical attributes that stick out, you need not own a yacht or private Lear jet, your parents don't have to be somebodies, and you certainly don't have to be gorgeous—or sane. In fact, the uglier, the dumber, and the more balls-out crazy you are, all the better! Not to beat up on the douche, but, again, Kevin Federline comes to mind!

Bloggywood is everywhere, and these days you don't even have to live in Hollywood. It's like you took our *Red Carpet Suidice* advice to heart and followed our lead. Because some of the most famous people in America right now weren't even a blip on the radar screen two years ago—or even a year ago. It seems like becoming a faux-lebrity was as easy as trying a few of these little press whore-y tactics:

★ Father eight children and become totally uninterested in your family as the entire world watches.

WOOD

★ Date a father of eight children who is totally uninterested in his family.

★ Mother eight children at ONCE! Combine them with the other six children you already had one at a time.

★ Flip a dinner table and call a supposed friend a "prostitute" and "whore."

★ Become governor of Alaska after serving a short term on a small-town council. Then leap right onto the Republican Party presidential ticket.

★ Seek treatment for sex addiction on a reality show and star in a "naked tape" with a TV star and his wife.

★ Boink the New York governor in exchange for sizable wads of traceable cash.

★ Die in the "trusted" care of your cardiologist. (Oh, let's be honest: Michael hadn't been a celebrity in years! The only way he got in the magazines and on the blogs and TV shows was to die. As I said in my first book, *Red Carpet Suicide*, sometimes you need to just die to be famous.)

But a lot of smack was talked about
me using the word in such a hateful
manner when I called
Black Eyed Peas "singer"
will.i.am a faggot.

Will.I.Am
Stoopid!

Another way to get noticed is to publicly call someone the "F" word. At the time, I thought, hey, I can say that. I mean, I am one. But a lot of smack was talked about me using the word in such a hateful manner when I called Black Eyed Peas "singer" will.i.am a faggot. Looking back, I realize things should have gone much differently the night I was assaulted in front of the Cobra Club. Earlier that evening, Lady Gaga and I had just attended Toronto's MuchMusic Awards, where BEP performed. Everyone was having a good time and leaving the Canadian hot spot at a reasonable predawn hour. Then, quicker than the JoBro/Taylor Swift breakup, will.i.am's all up in my panties about my Fugly posts. He's mad, I'm mad, and his team starts attacking me. I didn't mean it, I wish I hadn't done it, but I did. And while calling him a faggot was probably the wrong move at the time, the word takes a lot less serious tone when used here.

Wifey

PEREZ HILTON'S TRUE BLOGGYWOOD STORIES

I'm not suggesting it's okay for gay people to go around saying, "What's up, fag?" like the "N" word or anything like that. Not sayin', just sayin'.

While the true stories behind celebrity were exposed over the last few years, we learned that certain things aren't really all that intrinsic to being a celebrity, like weird baby names, pet pedicures, or $100,000 gold Balenciaga leggings. Where the average American used to sit back as Tom Hanks and Tom Cruise flashed their megawatt mouths on the red carpet in front of throngs of lens-wielding paparazzi, we as citizens of the blogosphere have lured the paparazzi off the red carpet and into real America. We figured out that we actually can be just as interesting as Jude Law or Colin Farrell. We just need to do wildly inappropriate things. And all the paps had to do is look for the same desperate, clawing need for attention so integral to the psyches of top-tier celebrities, unearth it in regular people, and then turn them into celebrities. It wasn't fame or millions that brought you notoriety anymore. You could be a call girl who slept with the governor of New York, and Diane Sawyer could lock you up for a prime-time exclusive interview. Ashley Dupré, aka "Spitzer's Girl," did just that. Famous? Sure. For more than fifteen minutes? Doubtful. And isn't it interesting how after more than a year later, still no book or TV movie deal? Hmmm. Someone once told me she probably got paid a lot more to "not tell all" than she would have been paid to actually tell all.

Another case in point: When was the last time you cared about Rebecca Gayheart? Wait. Let me rephrase that: Who is Rebecca Gayheart? Come on, think. You know this one. Right! The Noxzema girl in the early nineties. Because even

with her "leaked" sex tape with husband, McSteamy, and decrowned Miss Teen USA turned alleged madam, Kari Ann Peniche, we still didn't technically care about her. After all, it was still called "McSteamy's sex tape." But it sure got her in the news for once. Bloggywood brought you a lot of new celebrities and stars who weren't famous for anything other than earned fame. Sound familiar? Yup. The Rebecca Gayhearts, Bristol Palins, and Michael Phelpses of the world have eclipsed the bimbo blondes who rocked Hollywood just a few years earlier.

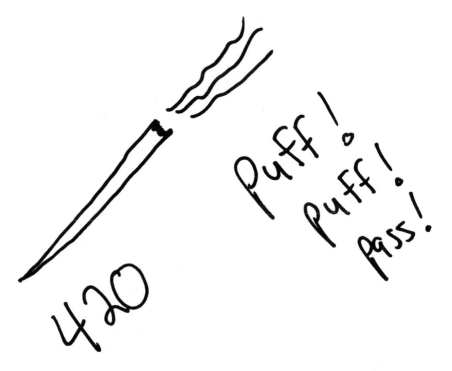

So where were Brad and Angelina, Tom and Katie, Jen, and Jessica while all of this was going on? Well, they were still doing their thing. Procreating (Brad and Angelina, NOT Jen,

ha ha), feigning true love (oh, give it up, TomKat!), and getting dumped (thanks, Jessica, we'll be able to write about you getting dumped in every book we ever write!).

But putting the A-listers and Faux-celebrities aside for a bit, this past year rolled out the red carpet for a new set of celebrities. Vampires, wife beaters, lesbians, presidents, womanizers, ex–*Playboy* bunnies, oh my! Lots of biting and lots of licking, that's for sure. It's a refreshing change from nipple flashes and disfiguring plastic surgeries, no? My prediction that you only had to do twelve simple steps to become famous was actually more true this past year than I ever thought it would be.

I mean who really gave a fuck about SaMANtha Ronson before she started licking Licksy Lohan? Mischa Barton became famous again—but this time NOT for playing a neurotic rich girl on TV but for actually being one. What was the real story

SNATCH

LezLo   SA MAN

I mean who really gave a fuck about SaMANtha Ronson before she started licking Licksy Lohan?

behind Barfton's breakdown of nuclear proportions just days before she was to return to acting and TV in *The Beautiful Life*. We have our opinions, of course; though Mushy and her team will brush it off with claims of "stress" or "exhaustion," like they all do, we know what's up here. There was a meaty rumor floating around Hollywood for years that Mischa once totally lost it in front of tons of celebrities of the Nicole Richie variety at a party. According to sources, the waif-y actress freaked out from eating too many magical mushrooms. Oopsie!

'WOOD

||||||||||||||||||||||||||||||||||||||||||||||||||||||||||||||||||||||||||||||||

Paris parties in other parts of the world (Dubai is so hawt) because no one pays attention to her in America anymore.

||||||||||||||||||||||||||||||||||||||||||||||||||||||||||||||||||||||||||||||||

In the old days we'd have been watching Paris Hilton crying in the backseat of a cop car or we'd have been glued to the screen as Britney got carted off in a stretcher to the loony bin. But things have gotten tame. Paris parties in other parts of the world (Dubai is so hawt) because no one pays attention to her in America anymore. Nicole Richie had a baby (and a hamburger); therefore her life has become increasingly less interesting in my eyes. Lindsay Lohan traded peen for poon, and it just doesn't leave the same taste in my mouth—or SaMANtha's, for that matter. She dated down—I hate to say it—and that caused her stardom to drop like McSteamy's drawers. Does anyone even care if she's going to be in a movie with Robert DeNiro? Well, if she royally screws it up, we sure will!

So here we are. A quiet Paris, a homely Nicole, a content Brad and Angelina, a single Jen—it's like everything we worked so hard for years just went out the window and left us to start from scratch. Where's Tired Reid when you need her? Well, she's still traipsing the world in hooker shoes, hosting parties for $1,500 a night, and getting wasted—but no one cares to even write about her poor saggy boobs anymore. I guess we're just so

ANOREXIC AND HOT!   HEALTHY AND BORING!

immune to her partying that it's not even worth acknowledging anymore.

Well, I refuse to give up on celebrity. So I, along with all of you, created new ones. New idols, new gods to drag down. Sure the pedestal that they all sit on is way lower down and more attainable than it should ever be for celebrity status—but considering that most of today's biggest celebrities don't even live in Hollywood (you probably don't either!), that's not a real shocker. Robert Pattinson, Jon and Kate Gosselin, Octomom—these people were all normal just like you a few years ago. But they all got really lucky, or unlucky in some cases, and something caused an entire nation to pay attention to them. Was it our hunger for bad things to happen

to other people so WE'D feel better about our boring lives, crappy job situations, and unsatisfying relationships?

You could be an absolute nobody and, in a flash, get your fifteen minutes faster and easier than ever. It's happening right now— with the Web and YouTube and Google and cell phones (we've said it before and we're saying it again), anyone can be famous if you get up off your ass and give it a go. Think about all of the reality shows on all of the networks on cable (and, counting Susan Boyle, technically all over the world). Even ESPN and the Travel Channel have reality shows now. There're probably more than a hundred networks and with close to five hundred reality shows. Some shows have anywhere from ten to two hundred contestants. You've probably got a better chance of ending up on a reality show than you do sleeping with someone in Obama's administration. And reality is by far the best way to try to become famous. Ask Jason Mesnick and Melissa Rycroft, two thoroughly uninteresting people from a seemingly dead reality show that was barely getting ratings. And all he had to do was propose to her, then dump her for that preppy twat, Molly Malaney. (Who dumps a smokin' former Dallas Cowboy cheerleader for an uptight blonde in plaid shorts?) And do it all on national TV. Talk about great TV! Talk about wanting to be famous. Well, that's one way to do it. Of course, he got famous by doing that, but the bachelorette got famous for getting dumped— which in turn landed her a gig on *Dancing with the Stars*! Nice one.

You've probably got a better chance of ending up on a reality show than you do sleeping with someone in Obama's administration.

BLOGG

**Maybe it was the great recession.
Maybe we all got sick of hearing that
Posh Spice bought another $8,000
Hermès Birkin bag
(but this one's orange).**

Maybe it was the great recession. Maybe we all got sick of hearing that Posh Spice bought another $8,000 Hermès Birkin bag (but this one's orange) or that Jay Leno added another luxury automobile to his lot of eighty-four cars and seventy-three motorcycles.

Don't even get me started on John Travolta with the jet and private runway he has in his front yard—are you kidding me? Then there're Will Smith and Jada talking about their sex life to make us think that they are just the übercelebrities they

Recession!

aren't. "When you have three kids," gushed Mrs. Smith to the press, "you've got to take your opportunities when they come. In a limo, on the way to the Academy Awards this year, Will started looking at me in this way that drives me wild. We started kissing passionately, and the next thing I knew—well, let's just say we missed the red carpet and I ended up with almost no makeup on." There's no way that's for real, so I don't blame the public for getting tired of all of that BS. Who wants to hear Will and

Jay Leno added another luxury automobile to his lot of eighty-four cars and seventy-three motorcycles.

Jada lie about their sex life? I don't. Plus, Robert Pattinson is so much hotter than any of those people.

So there we are. New people, new stars, old scandals applied to new victims. But that doesn't mean all the old A-listers have packed their Louis Vuitton luggage and left Bloggywood. Someone like Angelina Jolie is that much more important because we realize the value of her celebrity as compared to that of her peers. Sorry to say, but I don't see J.Lo or Tom Cruise or Will Smith anywhere on this list. Nope. We're over them. If J.Lo has another set of twins or Tom divorces Katie, maybe then I'd care. If Tom Cruise is out, what have we become? It certainly doesn't help him that he's married to *So You Think You Can Dance* guest star Katie Holmes. The two of them (plus Suri) are actually perfect together; they look like they belong in a J. Crew catalogue. Nice, but boring, and why buy something anyone can have?

The absence of heavy hitters like Tom Cruise from Bloggywood's spotlight has paved the way for a slew of others ready to take the crown of top celebrity status. After lifting the veil on Hollywood, it's become plain obvious that Julia Roberts, Gwyneth Paltrow, Harrison Ford, Lindsay Lohan, and Paris Hilton are barely even newsworthy anymore. Why? Well, what do they do? Gwyneth runs her how-to Web site, Goop.com, Julia's movies don't do well at the office, Gwyneth doesn't generate buzz. If all of these people were sitting in a Starbucks, would you rather go up and talk to one of them or Robert Pattinson? Or Obama? Or even Octomom! Okay, I'd probably want to slap Octomom for being the most irresponsible parent this side of David Hasselhoff, but I'd still rather go up to her and slap her than say hi to Gwyneth Paltrow. Hollywood has changed. Fame has changed. And with that change has come a new group of people WE ACTUALLY GIVE A SHIT ABOUT.

But it's also allowed us to cut through the smokescreen of celebrity. Celebrities have certainly let their guard down. Brad Pitt tells Bill Maher he's stopped smoking pot because he's a dad now. Jessica Simpson says she wants to marry Tony and have kids with him, then breaks up with him! Taylor Swift told Ellen DeGeneres that her JoBro dumped her by cell phone in a glib twenty-seven seconds. Celebs are speaking out more than ever in interviews, and they are letting their guard down. The REAL celebs are coming through. And the newbies like Jon Gosselin and Nadya Suleman have no idea how to handle it all, making it really easy for us to dig up dirt and figure out what the hell is going on. And thank our slutty stars for that.

Speaking of celebrities speaking out more, none other than everyone's favorite douche bag did just that on the 2009 MTV VMA's, creating a media frenzy that people are still talking about till this day! Kanye jumping on the stage and stealing innocent fawn Taylor Swift's moment and proclaiming Beyoncé to be the real winner was by far one of the best scandals that went down on national TV. After the debacle, all media headlines were showcasing Kanye's douchy act, and everyone including President Obama was calling the singer a "jackass." But did it hurt his sales? His image? No! It helped. The moment became his and it allowed him to "reflect" and "apologize," "comeback" and "reinvent" himself. This was the perfect plan for someone who had already reached the pinnacle of celebrity. He fabricated and engineered his own fall and demise—so all he can do is climb right back up. Genius.

And Beyoncé's class act later that night by giving Taylor the spotlight when Beyoncé won best video of the year made our eyes swell with tears. It almost made us want to take back all those times of calling her "Beyowulf." And what about Lady Gaga's VMA costumes? The bloody suicide performance. *The Phantom of the Opera* getup, the full face mask of red lace, the feather hat head, the feathers. Lady Gaga proved how being the worst dressed in Hollywood ultimately lands you the best-dressed award. The height of drama and spectacle that erupted that night is definitely going to be hard to top.

And, in a year full of deaths, from Farrah to Michael, it seems the one that saddened everyone without controversy was Patrick Swayze's. With Farrah videotaping her last days, and Michael's mysterious and shocking murder, his was a quiet passing. He went gracefully, defying the odds for several months when the *National Enquirer* said he only had weeks to live. In his last few weeks, his every move was documented (not by his choice)— even shots of him toking weed! Like a true Hollywood star! We'll miss you dearly, "Johnny Castle"! You showed that there is heart and soul in Hollywood after all.

TOP 10 CELEBRITIES OF OUR GENERATION

AND HOW THEY STAY RELEVANT

I'm not trying to be Barbara Walters here. There are no surprise guests. No prostitutes who slept with governors, no Olympic swimmers, no Jamie Foxx—just the best of the rest—the celebrities of 2009 who shocked and enthralled us all. Like Nadya Suleman. She actually insists she's never had plastic surgery. Uh, right. And David Hasselhoff is a stable parent. But it wasn't allllll Octomom. Not everyone had to spread their legs to get famous. In fact, our fan favorites still brought us a little bit of action throughout the year. Even some celebrities who were already famous got a little bit more famous as the year went on. Everyone knew who

Rihanna was from her music, but we weren't obsessively scoping the blogs for her whereabouts until the Chris Brown beatdown. Likewise, I don't think the average American could have picked Chris Brown out of a lineup—even though that's where he belongs! I'm not sure anyone outside of a country music bar knew who Mindy McCready was until her suicide attempt. But these aren't the most interesting or most fascinating people. Chris Brown needs to do a lot more than get in a scuffle with his girlfriend to intrigue me. I wouldn't say Megan Fox is the "next" anything. I'm not sure I'm so newsworthy either, but others seem to think that—especially every time I open my mouth. Farrah Fawcett didn't do anything to deserve fame other than die. It's sad, yeah, but I'm not sure we actually cared about her until we found out she was sick and dying. Were we regularly talking about her until then? So, for the most part, these people aren't actually captivating. They're just famous for the things they did, the fights they started, the things they said, and the places they went—and why we loved and/or hated them.

So in no particular order . . . I give you the newest top ten celebrities who really count:

EGO

EGO

Yo R-PATZ,
I'm really happy for you
and imma let you finish,
but Brad Pitt was one
of the hottest vampires
of all time. BEST!

★ Robert Pattinson ★

Dirty
Sexy

Let's start with his jawline. No, wait: his hair (product). Or how about the way he pushes up one eyebrow with his finger when he's trying to think of something to say? Sigh. He's just

||||||||||||||||||||||||||||||||||||||||

But when Rpatz is in sight, the girls go absolutely bananas.

||||||||||||||||||||||||||||||||||||||||

got this crazy effect over girls that Leonardo DiCaprio HAD ten years ago. Girls still think Leo is hot, but they definitely don't go all gaga and wet their Team Leo panties when they see him. Because no one makes Team Leo anything. But when Rpatz is in sight, the girls go absolutely bananas. B-A-N-A-N-A-S! Like Leo, Rob has aspirations to do more meaningful things. He wants to act in real movies, not just be a brooding vampire who can't bite the one chick he wants to bite (even if offscreen he's doing a little more than biting!). If DiCaprio was able to do it, so can Pattinson. Leo segued from *Growing Pains* to *Titanic*, *Blood Diamond*, *Catch Me If You Can*, and more. Dare I say that Rpatz has more of a shot at having a longer career than the sekstastic Zac Efron? Zac woulda coulda shoulda been huge . . . had he done *Footloose*! But instead he is doing *Me and Orson Welles*. Oh, how I'd rather have seen him kick off those Sunday blues in *Footloose*. Anyway, what ties Leo, Rpatz, and Zac all together? The boyishly rakish good looks? Nope! The gay rumors! But I don't think Pattinson's gay. He's not gay. Just rumors. I wish. And I sure hope for Kristen Stewart's sake he's not. If he were, I'd date him. (I really need to get myself a celebrity boyfriend.)

As if you needed any more proof for why this guy is in the top ten, here goes: Any guy who has millions of people talking nonstop about his hair is definitely worthy of being on the list of interesting people. And remember when he went shirtless in Europe while filming *New Moon*? They were like the photos seen around the world! ROBERT PATTINSON. SHIRT-

LESS. OMG! It was a bigger deal than when the Obamas got a puppy. And then everyone started speculating if the abs were real or airbrushed. I mean, REALLY? Is that what we've come to? We speculate on whether the guy's abs are real or fake or whatever. Again, that's when you know you've made it. Well, news flash: They spray-painted a lot of the abs on in *Twilight*. But who cares? I need to do that. We should all do that. But here's what makes Robert Pattinson so intriguing: If you saw

Robert Pattinson on the street and he wasn't famous, you probably wouldn't even look twice. A tall, pale British dude with a little boy's chest? You wouldn't even blink. But throw in his "Edward" character and all of a sudden every girl and fag in the world wants to jump his eternal bones.

CONSPIRACY THEORY

Robert and Kristen keep it interesting by NEVER acknowledging their relationship. They like to run their hands through their hair and act like they are struggling with this newfound fame as if they don't want any of it. They don't deny they are dating. They don't acknowledge they are dating. Entire months have gone by with rotating covers on every tabloid claiming they're on or they're not on. They just play along with it, and the intrigue makes them that much bigger.

Robert and Kristen keep it interesting by NEVER acknowledging their relationship.

★ Barack Obama ★

A gay man almost won *American Idol* but an African-American did win the presidency! WOW. I did vote for him . . . eventually. In the primary I voted for Hillary Clinton. I'm not so sure how I'd vote now. More important, look at the attention we lavished upon our new president, as opposed to his predecessor. We bow down to this guy. We quaked with anticipation for Inauguration Day like it was the opening of a Brad Pitt movie. His image generates more shwag than Clint Eastwood and Tupac Shakur combined. Obama definitely has

worked hard to keep himself in the spotlight (that's why he's one of the top ten celebrities!). He had so many press conferences in his first year! More than any other president during his first year in office, which wasn't as glowing an introduction as many would have hoped for him. Oh and let me just say it loud and clear—his absence in the fight for gay rights. Even with Obama in office, gays still can't get legally married everywhere. So I give him a grade of "F." And that F is not for "faggot." And certainly not for "fabulous." It's for "fuck that."

CONSPIRACY
THEORY

It's definitely not that he secretly supports Al-Qaeda or lied about his daughter's allergies to justify getting a purebred puppy. It's that Obama has very serious ambitions about influencing the American public through the use of his star power. He knows that as soon as he took office, the question on everyone's mind the very next day was "What's he doing right now?" We wish we could have a constant stream of video showing him dining out with friends and playing fetch with Bo, but he's the president, so we have to settle for his casual public appearances courtside at basketball games and out on dates with his pretty, stylish wife. We eat up how cool and normal he seems. Then, when he wants to get his way and he knows Congress is going to give him a hard time, he gets on TV.

★ Octomom ★

■ ■ ■ ■ ■ ■ ■ ■ ■ ■ ■ ■

I think people are interested in her because it's a double-edged-sword situation: She's a real, everyday person, but she's also a freak.

■ ■ ■ ■ ■ ■ ■ ■ ■ ■ ■ ■

I gotta say one thing about Nadya Suleman: She's still around. She's a hot mess, but she's still around. Who'd have thought a homely single mom would become the most talked-about person of the year? I think people are interested in her because it's a double-edged-sword situation: She's a real, everyday person, but she's also a freak. It works on both levels. At first I was thinking, "Good Lord, how wide is this woman's vagina?"—but then I remembered she had a C-section. Her lips are probably wider than her vagina. Speaking of her lips, don't buy into anything she says—she's definitely obsessed with Angelina Jolie. And you know who is paying for all of this? We are. Should we be? Hell no! Our taxes will be paying for this nut job and her kids for the next eighteen years! No way can she make enough money playing "Octo-mom" on reality TV to raise fourteen kids for eighteen years. She might make money for the next eight years or decade—selling weekly access to her family to the *National Enquirer* or RadarOnline.com for a few thousand dollars a week. She did deals with RadarOnline.com and sold her life stories to tabloids through various photo agencies. But for how long will people care? Doubtfully through the orthodontia years. Will Ann Curry be there for the octuplets' high school graduation? Maybe. Will Katie Couric interview them come law school time? I don't think so. Those kids won't be going to law school! McDonald's drive-thru is more like it. But they won't be commanding money by then. And PS—remember, "Octo"-mom has fourteen children! People forget about the six other kids. For a single mom who doesn't get along with her own mom and doesn't have a job, this isn't going to turn out well. At some point she's going to crack.

Her lips are probably wider than her vagina.

CONSPIRACY THEORY

Did she plan living close by to LA? Would she have been as famous had she lived anywhere else? It's interesting to point out—one of the reasons why the Octomom story blew up and became a big phenomenon was because of her close proximity to Los Angeles. Think about it—she lives just east of LA in Whittier, California. So all of these news crews paid attention to her and blew the story up. They didn't have to go out of town and fly to some remote town in Nebraska. No news team in their right mind would pay to continually fly out their crews to Nebraska—especially in a recession! But Whittier? Shizz, that's like thirty minutes away! She has luck and geography to thank for being one of the big stars of 2009. It was very easy to cover her story.

★ Jon Gosselin ★ and Kate Gosselin

The real JK8 die-hards already knew Kate was a bitch and controlling and emasculating. I'm on neither side for this one. Well, I'm on the kids' side. I call it "Side 8" for the eight kids. I feel bad for them having to perform on TV.

The Gosselin 8

Busted! That's how it all started. *Us Weekly* plastered them on the cover saying Jon was stepping out on Kate and then BAM! They were dunzo. They are great because just like Octomom they are freaks, but they seem like a normal suburban family, or at least they pretended to be normal better than Nadya. You can only keep a freak on lockdown for so long. So, did she drive him mad? Is he just an immature asshole? Kate's not unlike Octomom in that she did have all these kids too. Their relationship and dynamic were already under fire from fans

Property of
Kate Gosselin

Jon's balls

of the show. The real JK8 diehards already knew Kate was a bitch and controlling and emasculating. I'm on neither side for this one. Well, I'm on the kids' side. I call it "Side 8" for the eight kids. I feel bad for them having to perform on TV. I get it if maybe four or five of them WANT to be on TV. But I'll bet not all of them do. And they are forced to. Every day of their young lives captured on TV. Did you know that some days neither Kate nor Jon is there to supervise the kids' tapings? Sometimes it's just the producers and nannies. Isn't that illegal? I don't know. I do know that Jon is a complete d-bag. Make no mistake, Jon Gosselin is the 2009 Douche of the Year. It doesn't matter whether it's his midlife crisis or one-third-life crisis (he's not that old yet) because he needs to man up and grow some balls and take care of his kids. I mean the guy's fooling around on his wife publicly, getting caught, dating losers, wearing tacky clothes, smoking like a chimney. All of a sudden he's smoking a lot and it's his idea of cool. He's dating girls who have been arrested for drugs and hanging out with big-time loser Michael Lohan. That's not cool, dude. That's just totally lame.

|||||||||||||||||||||||||||||||||||||||||||||||||||||||

Kate Gosselin has the reverse mullet! Everyone is talking about her hair. There is nothing new or original about her hair. I know, because I've had that do! I was Pre–Kate Gosselin, y'all.

|||||||||||||||||||||||||||||||||||||||||||||||||||||||

While Jon and Kate are the epitome of lame, they are also at the apex of fame. And one of the reasons they are famous: Kate's hair. I said it in my last book—lots of celebs have their "thing"—the one attribute they are known for. Larry King has his suspenders, Jay Leno has his chin, Hugh Hefner has his robe—well, Kate Gosselin has the reverse mullet! Everyone is talking about her hair. There is nothing new or original about her hair. I know, because I've had that do! I was Pre–Kate Gosselin, y'all.

At the 2008 Grammys, I had that hair. For real. Kate Gosselin has Perez Hilton hair! She had a lot of gravitas this year and appeared on way too many talk shows. How many times was she on the cover of *Us Weekly*—probably close to ten times, I think. They'll be done soon enough. The ratings of their show tanked after everyone realized they split. It's possible that by the time this book prints, you won't even care about them anymore. And if that's the case, thank God.

Everyone knows the marriage was over way before *Us Weekly* busted them. So they were definitely faking it for the cameras. If they were capable of faking a marriage prior to the official split, it kind of makes you wonder what fakery they've been up to since? How is it that every photographer knows where they will be? We'll get to that soon enough, my bitches.

CONSPIRACY THEORY

BLOGG

She's our A-lister who keeps it going strong. Even minor details, like which career moves she makes, are mildly interesting. So why don't we care about Tom Cruise but still obsess over Angelina? Well, check this one out: The lead role in the movie with a working title of *Salt* was originally written for a man to be played by Tom Cruise. But Angelina Jolie read the script and decided she wanted to do the movie. So the producers rewrote the script for a female. Cruise was out; Jolie was in. It was that easy for her! I mean, how the hell do you steal a role from Tom Cruise? Apparently nowadays you just do! That just goes to show you that Tom Cruise is out (no, not THAT kind of "out," silly bitches) and Jolie is in.

She's our A-lister who keeps it going strong. Even minor details, like which career moves she makes, are mildly interesting.

CONSPIRACY THEORY

If Tom Cruise gets shot by the paps only when he summons them, then it's safe to say the same goes for Jolie. She knows that all the rumors flying around about her fighting with Brad are good for her career in the end.

★ Megan Fox ★

||||||||||||||||||||||||||||||||||||||||||||||||||||||

Megan Fox is
the new Angelina.

||||||||||||||||||||||||||||||||||||||||||||||||||||||

She was on the cover of practically every magazine. She was in the biggest movies and on the most Web sites—it was definitely the year of Megan "the Fox." Plus, she gives great sound bites. Observe: "My wardrobe on *Transformers* always smells like farts, and I have no idea why." She's crazy and loves talking about sex and men and women and relationships. If you're a celebrity and want to be talked about, you have to talk about sex. That's just standard. She starred in one of the biggest movies of the year, *Transformers*. Everyone's saying she's the new Angelina Jolie, except her, because she says she's scared of Jolie's power and would be embarrassed to meet her. Still, she may very well knock Angelina off the list next year. If you think about it, she's just a younger, sexier version! *Details* and *GQ* and *Elle*—they all wanted her this year. Megan gets people talking. I think she's realistic and knows she's not the greatest actress, and while she's not the next big Oscar winner and probably never will be, she's actually very talented. She knows her limits. She's hot, and that always goes very far in Hollywood. She's even keeping everyone on her feet with the Brian Austin Green situation. She's just playing the B.A.G. situation. The second she blows up, it's like she can't admit she's with him. For him it's probably a struggle; he's probably insecure now that she's become Megan Fox! When they first started dating, she was a nobody and he was Brian Austin Green! But now she's Megan Fox and he's the nobody. It's just like Ryan Phillippe and Reese Witherspoon. She really is like Angelina in many ways. With her big action movies, wild-child image, tattoos, and sultry body, she's the raven-haired beauty who's gonna steal your man. Even if she is just standing near another guy, there are going to be rumors. She once stood with Zac Efron, and immediately reports surfaced that Vanessa Hudgens didn't want Zac talking to her. That doesn't happen with Angelina anymore. Because Megan Fox is the new Angelina.

CONSPIRACY THEORY

Megan Fox has so much more appeal when she's single! Ever notice how right when her star is rising, she "splits" with Brian Austin Green—but then they show up in photos together, have dinner or lunch, pick each other up at the airport? Yeah. Welcome to Hollywood. I believe they are still "secretly" together, but they need to maintain "single" status so Megan's selling point—her sex appeal—is still intact.

BLOGG

I thought he was faking a heart attack to get out of his London shows.

I have to admit, when Michael first died I didn't believe it. I was skeptical. What can I say? And I got called out for it. Here's a guy who wore a mask for the better part of the last decade of his life, didn't have a nose, had massive amounts of plastic surgery, and was, for the most part, a recluse from all of society except for Las Vegas bookstore parking lots or Bahrain palaces. I say what's on people's minds. I thought he was faking a heart attack to get out of his London shows. Consensus in the industry is that he wouldn't have been able to perform fifty shows. Plus, he has a history of pulling out of things! He pulled out of an HBO special in the nineties, showed up late to court hearings, if at all, and then when he did, he was wearing his PJ's. So I thought he was faking it. That's my job: to determine and interpret rumors and information. What can I say? It was all just a matter of unfortunate timing. It went from initial reports that he was being rushed to the hospital (which I subsequently posted online, cautiously) to IT'S SERIOUS, PEOPLE in like fifteen minutes. Once I knew he wasn't faking, I changed my initial post because it all happened within like twenty to twenty-five minutes. I went from giving my opinion to giving the facts. He was dead. It wasn't a lot of time that elapsed, so I felt like I had to change it. I wasn't trying to be deceitful by changing my original post. I was trying to NOT

MICHAEL JACKSON

Tragedy

ʃ ʃ L L

MJ's
nose

MJ's
nose
in 100
years

mislead anyone once I got the facts straight. It was crazy, sad, and unfortunate. How crazy? Well, that month of June was the most visited month of my Web site ever. The day of his death, I had a lot of readers, even more than the day when Heath Ledger died, which had been my previous record, and even more than the first Brad and Angelina "spotted together" photos, which crashed my site more than five years ago. In June, because of Michael Jackson, I got almost 300 million page views. But I stand by what I did in terms of not believing the heart attack was real, initially, and making fun of it. If this were happening to Lindsay Lohan, I'd probably be saying the same thing. She'd be claiming some kind of "dehydration," and I would make fun of her, because I would assume she's probably lying, that it was probably drugs. Like we've seen a million times before. If she dies, I'd be sad. I'm not going to take it easy on her though initially. I'd say the first thing that comes to my mind. I didn't do the wrong thing on Michael Jackson. I'd do it again. It was just unfortunate timing. When Bernie Mac was hospitalized right before he died, I said, "I hope you're not faking it, Bernie!" He died days later. I didn't go back and change the post. Because that was two days later, not thirty minutes later. When Michael died, fans on Twitter attacked me. Ashlee Simpson attacked me on Twitter pretty harshly. But what people don't get about celebrity is that earlier that day I had uploaded a hideous post on Asslee and her new plump lips. She was actually more pissed at me for that, and used me as a

PEREZ HILTON'S TRUE BLOGGYWOOD STORIES

scapegoat, saying I was wrong to call Michael Jackson a faker. Whatever. It's Asslee. She's got a kid at home she ought to be taking care of and a husband she needs to be pleasing. She shouldn't have time to pick on me. But I'm glad the celebs pick on me. Just makes me that much bigger.

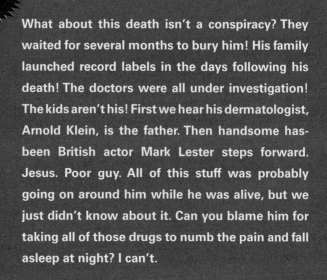

CONSPIRACY THEORY

What about this death isn't a conspiracy? They waited for several months to bury him! His family launched record labels in the days following his death! The doctors were all under investigation! The kids aren't his! First we hear his dermatologist, Arnold Klein, is the father. Then handsome has-been British actor Mark Lester steps forward. Jesus. Poor guy. All of this stuff was probably going on around him while he was alive, but we just didn't know about it. Can you blame him for taking all of those drugs to numb the pain and fall asleep at night? I can't.

WOOD

★ Farrah Fawcett ★

Poor Farrah Fawcett! As if it weren't bad enough that she had anal cancer, the day she dies—the day SHE'S supposed to get her big *People* magazine cover—Michael Fucking Jackson dies, too! It's bye-bye, Farrah. Hello, Michael, Dr. Murray, Jermaine, Blanket, and Miko Brando! But regardless of the quickness of America's mourning period over her death, it was definitely her year. She spent the last years of her life battling cancer, and as if it weren't bad enough having her final days splashed across the cover of the *National Enquirer*, she then let NBC cameras follow her for an NBC special chronicling her pain, life, and treatment. PS: Poor Ed McMahon! He was eclipsed by Farrah. Anyway, she was America's pin-up, with the hair, the boobs, *Charlie's Angels*. One of the only times in 2009 I actually watched a whole TV show was during her documentary special. We did a lot of death watching in 2009.

> **But regardless of the quickness of America's mourning period over her death, it was definitely her year.**

The Natasha Richardson death we watched for days. We discussed whether we should wear helmets while skiing. We watched as Liam Neeson grieved. We learned the names of her kids (then later forgot them). But Farrah's was so much more of a drawn-out situation. The same thing happened in the UK with their beloved reality star Jade Goody. We watched her final days on earth. We knew her more when she was bald and sick than we did when she was alive and healthy. Because as entertainment, unfortunately, she became more interesting that way. SICK! That's so gross of us, but it's true. We were watching people die in front of our eyes for our own morbid entertainment. The

worst joke I heard all year was . . . Question: What do Farrah Fawcett and Michael Jackson want for Christmas? Answer: Patrick Swayze. Horrible. Horrible. Horrible. As the world became intrigued by the deaths of Farrah, Michael, Jade, and Patrick Swayze, reality TV finally hit that place. Makes you wonder, where to next?

★ Perez Hilton ★

That's right. I'm putting myself on my own list. What can I say? This has been the most eventful year of my life. It was filled with good and bad, and either way, it was definitely interesting. I've had so many highs. I released my first ever book in January. I released my second book in December. Two books in one year! Irish twins! And I'm happy with both! I launched a record label, produced my first music tour, introduced new artists to the world, and started CocoPerez, my fashion blog. I opened up Britney's big Circus show to the world. I was amidst headlines for Miss USA, will.i.am, Michael Jackson, Dustin Lance Black, and the Gay Rights Movement.

■ ■ ■ ■ ■ ■ ■ ■ ■ ■ ■ ■ ■

I opened up Britney's big Circus show to the world. I was amidst headlines for Miss USA, will.i.am, Michael Jackson, Dustin Lance Black, and the Gay Rights Movement.

■ ■ ■ ■ ■ ■ ■ ■ ■ ■ ■ ■ ■

Could I have peaked? I say that every year. If nothing else ever happens, I'm just happy. I read recently where a writer made a Paris Hilton comparison to me, that a few years ago she was more relevant than she is now and that eventually the same will happen to me. I keep waiting for that to happen, but my audience keeps growing and I keep getting into

G~~LAAD~~

NOT glaad

H.A.P.P.Y.

Homosexuals
And
Perverts
Protecting
You

HAPPY

Boo! booooo
           boooo
Booooo!

more trouble for what I say and do. The big difference between Paris and me is that I work harder; she doesn't work
consistently hard like I do. I am always hustling, always got
my grind on. Even in Japan, where I went while right in the
middle of writing this book, I barely slept because I was in
three different time zones: LA (my home-base time), NYC
(my Web time), and Japan. I'd like to think that at some point
in the future I will average a billion page views per month.
I'd like to see more and more and more. Oh, and I had my
weight loss. I vowed to lose a lot of weight at the beginning

of the year as my New Year's resolution. I don't weigh myself, so I don't know how much I lost, but I'd venture to say it was in the forty-pound range. Finally, I'm getting laid! I'm going out on dates. Many dates. And now I've got random hookups. I wonder if it's because I'm skinny now? That's kinda sad, if that's the case. I used to be skeptical of people dating me—I'd question their reasoning. But hey, if people use me, I'll use them right back. I won't date people who are using me, but I'll have sex with them! Ha. All I can say is thank goodness the drought is over.

||||||||||||||||||||||||||||||||||||||||||||||

Finally, I'm getting laid! I'm going out on dates. Many dates. And now I've got random hookups.

||||||||||||||||||||||||||||||||||||||||||||||

CONSPIRACY THEORY

I could tell you, but then I'd have to kill you.

★ Chris Brown ★

If he's hurting on the inside, he hasn't really shown it. You see him partying, clubbing, hanging out with other girls who look like Rihanna.

I choose him over Rihanna because he's the aggressor. He's the one who did the action. He's an asshole. If he's hurting on the inside, he hasn't really shown it. You see him partying, clubbing, hanging out with other girls who look like Rihanna. He didn't publicly apologize for months. Then he releases a statement/apology MONTHS too late, and it was so scripted and not authentic and completely unbelievable. AKA BULLSHIT. But at the same time in Hollywood, he might actually still have a future. Remember that dancing couple who, along with their whole wedding party, was dancing in the church aisles and it went viral on YouTube and eventually was featured on morning programs and covered in the mainstream press? The song they were dancing to: Chris Brown's "Forever." That utterly adorbs clip was the best PR Brown could have asked for. The guy makes good music and the public loves it. We shall see.

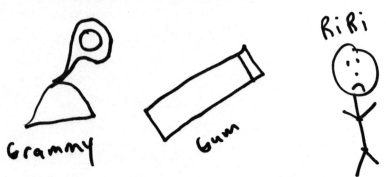

CONSPIRACY THEORY

While it is always wrong to hit someone, how many of us wondered who struck first? Rihanna looks like she could mess someone up pretty good if she wanted to. What if Chris was just trying to get his enraged, jealous pop-star girlfriend off of him? We might not ever know.

Stay Strong!

THE ANNUAL PEREZZIES

FOR EXCELLENCE IN ABSURDITY

While Hollywood gives out Oscars and Emmys, Bloggywood has found its own way of honoring its most revered and reviled offscreen acts. Whether it's young girls stripping for their boyfriends and texting them the photos (aka sending them out to the world so they can get more famous), beatings, overdoses, or just flat out getting dumped when everyone but you knew it would happen, celebrities deserve to be recognized for their outrageous behavior.

Therefore I give to you the first annual

PEREZZIES:

★ BEST NUDE PHOTO SCANDAL ★

You can never have enough tits, cock, and ass! Without it, Hollywood would just have drugs! But drugs and sexy photos often go together. Just ask Rebecca GAYheart-less. What is it about nude photo scandals that bring out more poon than peen? I guess guys aren't into showing off their goods as much as the bitches are. We saw some cock this year—we saw Michael Stipe playing flasher in the shower; we saw Eric Dane's peen flopping on the way to the hot tub. We saw some almost-poon a few times from Miley Cyrus, and of course everyone from Posh to Paris to Britney and Lindsay flashed us their beef curtains while getting out of various cars. In fact we saw the hoo-has of almost everyone in Hollywood—even Maniston—at some point this year—except Heidi Montag! And she posed for *Playboy*. Guess we always should have known that you do not always get your money's worth with Heidi Montag. So before someone like *Twilight*'s Ashley Greene gets caught up

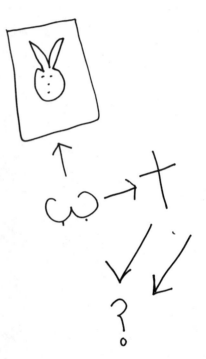

In fact we saw the hoo-has of almost everyone in Hollywood at some point this year—except Heidi Montag! And she posed for *Playboy*.

in a nude photo scandal—oh, too late, she already did—let's announce the nominations for the first annual Perezzie for NUDE PHOTO SCANDAL:

the nominations:

a. *Leighton Meester:* Did you know about this one? Not a lot of people did. Salacious photos AND an accompanying video hit the Web showing off this gorgeous Gossip Girl in all her glory. But was it really her? She says it wasn't! Whoever that was, the scandal went away either due to lack of interest or just some good legal work on the part of her lawyer! If it was her, she gives a mean hand job with her feet!

b. *Rihanna:* Just weeks after her bust up with Chris Brown, photos of her bust and ass ended up all over the Web. Looks like she took them herself or, even worse, in the presence of Chris Brown! Damn! Girl got screwed over twice.

c. *Dustin Lance Black:* The very out and gay writer of *MILK* got caught up in a nude photo scandal that was the topic of a lot of criticism. Why would I, an openly gay blogger, try to "take down" someone like Dustin, who was just having sex? Photos emerged of him at a party sticking it good to another guy. So I thought I'd post the photos—I mean that's what I do for a living, so why wouldn't I? Well, I didn't take him down. I didn't filter it. I did what I did for every other nude photo scandal: I posted the photos. I didn't treat him any differently, even if he wasn't wearing protection. A lot of the gay community didn't want me to show that; they didn't want me showing irresponsible, unprotected sex. But hey, it happened and I'm going to report on it. If you want filtered, rated-PG news, go buy *Reader's Digest*.

IIIIIIIIIIIIIIIIIIIIIIIIIIIIIIIIIIIIIIIIIIIIIIIIIII

Photos emerged of him at a party sticking it good to another guy. So I thought I'd post the photos—I mean that's what I do for a living, so why wouldn't I?

IIIIIIIIIIIIIIIIIIIIIIIIIIIIIIIIIIIIIIIIIIIIIIIIIII

d. *Vanessa Hudgens:* Not again, Vag-nessa. A few years ago Vanessa showed off her eager beaver in sexy, severely underaged nude photos that were supposedly "meant" for an ex-boyfriend. Zac Efron, maybe? Whoever they were for, about half of America ended up receiving them! And then she did it again. More nudie photos of Vanessa Hudgens rampage across the blogosphere! A lot of pervy old guys have seen Vanessa Hudgens naked more times than they've seen their own wives in their birthday suits!

WOOD

Vanexxxa's  tittays!

Again!

Whatshername's boobs!

And then she did it again. More nudie photos of Vanessa Hudgens rampage across the blogosphere! A lot of pervy old guys have seen Vanessa Hudgens naked more times than they've seen their own wives in their birthday suits!

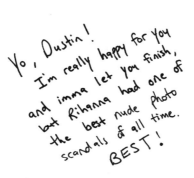

Yo, Dustin!
I'm really happy for you
and imma let you finish,
but Rihanna had one of
the best nude photo
scandals of all time.
BEST!

And the winner for the Best Nude Photo Scandal:

I ♥ Pictures!

Dustin Lance Black! This is Dustin's first Perezzie!
It's not my fault this guy had unprotected sex with some

guy and then let the guy take digital photos of it all. We've said it before: DO NOT TAKE PHOTOS OF YOURSELF NAKED OR HAVING SEX. It WILL come back to haunt you one day. I must say one thing though: We've come a long way, folks. It used to be that you had to be Paris Hilton or Vanessa Hudgens to get famous from a nude photo scandal. Not anymore! Now you can be a screenwriter and be known more for your cock and not your pen! The gay community might have thought I was doing them a disservice by posting the smutty shots. But that is so hypocritical. I'd be doing the gay community a disservice by blocking the photos. I'd basically be saying it's okay to run other shots of heterosexuals having sex but NOT when it's the homos. That's just wrong. I treat everyone the same. The guy was caught having unprotected sex! Shame on him for letting the photos be taken. If I was out to take him down, I could have said it wasn't his steady boyfriend. I'm not saying it now either—I'm just letting it be known people were trying to tell me that. A typical Sunday afternoon for Tommy Lee and Pam Anderson. But how's about that! And it was definitely a younger boy. He likes dating young boys. Definitely much younger. Also, I heard there was a third person in the room that no one knows about. Hey, fella, if you're out there reading this, e-mail me!

DO NOT TAKE PHOTOS OF YOURSELF NAKED OR HAVING SEX. It WILL come back to haunt you one day.

BLOGG

Hollywood is known for its action scenes. Typically we're talking about something with Jason Statham or Jet Li jumping off of buildings or crashing cars. But every once in a while we get REAL action that's caught on tape (grrrrrrrr, though not always) or goes further than in front of the camera. So here we have the Perezzie for BEST REAL-ACTION SCENE:

the nominations:

a. *Kate Gosselin* spanking her daughter. It made the cover of *In Touch* magazine when she smacked the shit out of that kid! Then she told *Life & Style*, "I love my children and when they misbehave, I discipline them as I deem appropriate for the situation." Ha!

b. *Chris Brown and Rihanna.* We all know what happened here. Reportedly, Rihanna saw some sexy "sext" messages on Chris's phone and went batshit before Chris turned around and beat her down. Oh, and don't forget this all happened in a Lamborghini—even if it was leased, talk about a Hollywood action scene.

c. *Lindsay Lohan and Samantha Ronson's scream-fests:* It's like every other night Lindsay would find herself outside of Sam's house screaming like a stray cat, "Let me in!" But Sam wouldn't budge. Usually

this would go on between the hours of one a.m. and three a.m. The photographers would get tired, go home, and then we'd see Lindsay emerge from Sam's house at nine a.m., walking a little funny.

d. *Brody Jenner and Joe Francis's bar fight:* They got into it over Jayde Nicole. It's so D-List and boring, I can't even believe I'm nominating this. Basically Jenner decides to defend the Playmate's honor after the *Girls Gone Wild* creator roughed her up at Hollywood hot spot Guys and Dolls. It was all over the Web the next day, and no one cared. I still don't think anyone could pick those guys out of a lineup. Beat up a Grammy-winning pop star under the tutelage of Jay-Z? Colossal shizzstorm. Smack a *Playboy* model? Ho-hum. The blogosphere tried, but no one bit.

And the winner for BEST REAL-ACTION SCENE is *Chris Brown and Rihanna!* This is the first Perezzie for both Chris and Rihanna. Rihanna was nominated once before in the Best Nude Photo Scandal. This was definitely the action scene that shocked most of the celeb watchers this year. The Grammys-bound pop couple left a pre-party thrown by big-time producer Clive Davis on February 8 and ended up somewhere near Rihanna's Hollywood Hills home when the fight broke out. Cops found a bruised and battered Rihanna and admitted her to Cedars-Sinai Medical Center for treatment of her injuries. I can't believe of all the absurd things that the paparazzi catch on camera, that they missed this one. Of all the times not to follow them. We get millions of boring videos of Lindsay Lohan wobbling in and out of clubs, Jen Aniston eating dinner at Il Sole, but we can't get the biggest dustup of the year? This easily was one of the biggest stories of the year in Hollywood because it transcended celebrity

lines. You know it's a big story when Wolf Blitzer and Brian Williams are leading off their lineups with this story. Do I condone violence like this? Absolutely not! Should Rihanna have listened? Of course! Ha. Kidding.

BLOGG

. . . and the award for biggest split goes to . . . Kirstie Alley's pants! Oh, wait. This isn't for biggest split? Ohhhhh, it's for MOST PREDICTABLE SPLIT. Sheesh. Well, yeah, in Hollywood you can always see a good split coming. Obviously, Pete and Ashlee are gonna end up in divorce court. No way are Brad and Angelina gonna last. Tom and Katie will definitely one day be dunzo. It happens to the best of them (even Paris & Doug and Kim & Reggie, oh my God!). Mel Gibson knocked up his girlfriend before he and his wife finally split the sheets for good. Now that Brandi Glanville has filed for divorce, her soon-to-be ex-hubby, Eddie Cibrian, is already publicly golfing with his not-so-secret lover, LeAnn Rimes. But until all of those people split, let's talk about the ones that did split. So the nominations for the Perezzi for the MOST PREDICTABLE SPLIT are:

the nominations:

a. *Jessica Simpson and Tony Romo:* Poor Jessica didn't even get to eat any wedding cake! Her sister is already married (not for long!) with a kid. We saw this one coming a mile away. Tony got all of the fame he wanted, and when that junk in the trunk just got to be too much, he threw Jessica Simpson like a football—and out of the stadium.

Poor Jessica didn't even get to eat any wedding cake!

b. *Jon and Kate Gosselin: Us Weekly* predicted this one! And after a few weeks of watching this family and marriage totally crumble in front of our eyes, it was obvious they weren't going to make it to number nine. Jon went on to stick his peen in anything with a pulse.

c. *Nick Lachey and Vanessa Minnillo:* Who fucking cares? I'm just naming them because they split. But this could also be nominated in the WHO GIVES A SHIT? SPLIT.

d. *Madonna and Guy:* She dumped him for A-Rod, then dumped A-Rod for a guy name Jesus! Madonna and Jesus? Isn't that incest or something? She's still got it, though; I gotta hand it to her.

e. *Amy and Blake:* Well, he was in jail for all that time. No one expected Wino to wait for him. Of course, the best part of their breakup is that as soon as the divorce is final and Blake's out of the pen, Ames sneaks him over to her place for a little makeup nookie. They tried to make her break up with Blake and she said, "No, no, no!"

And the winner for
MOST PREDICTABLE SPLIT:

Jessica Simpson and Tony Romo. Who didn't see this one coming? She was begging him for an engagement ring! The only ring Tony wanted was a Super Bowl ring, and that wasn't coming as long as he was dating Jinxica Simpson. Plus, Papa Joe Simpson was meddling in their business, showing up on their vacations and just being his usual douche-y self. There were rumors for months that Tony was cheating on his girlfriend of two years—even making passes at Jessica's friends. Did he? Doesn't matter. Where there's smoke, there's fire. The rumor on the street is that he pretty much dumped her on her birthday. She had a whole shindig planned, a big Ken and Barbie–themed soiree with Tony and Pete and Asslee and Momma and Poppa—but she had to cancel it! Poor Jessica! When will she learn? If she wants to find true love, she needs to find someone either more famous than she is (shouldn't be hard!) or move out of Hollywood and just be normal. That's how the rest of the world does it.

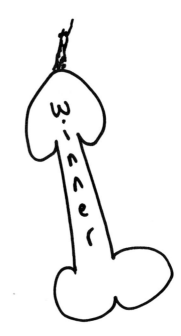

BLOGG

Do we have enough time to cover this category before we cut to a commercial? I don't want them cuing up the music before I'm done. But luckily we're only naming the last few boyfriends and not EVERYONE. I don't think we'd even have enough paper for that and all of the failed relationships. Plus, using that much paper to talk about Jen Aniston's boyfriends would be so bad for the environment! Oh, no, they're cuing the music! Okay, real quick—the nominations for the Perezzie for BEST JEN ANISTON BOYFRIEND:

the nominations:

a. *John Mayer*: Chronologically, John came after Jen ended things with Cameron Diaz's ex Paul Sculfor and after dating a production guy named Brian Bourma. John certainly seemed like the most legitimate of the bunch. But did we think they'd get married? Hellll noooo!!!! John Mayer married? Wait. Jen Aniston married? Maniston wishes! John still needs to make his "O-face" for at least another thousand girls.

b. *Bradley Cooper*: What a cute couple they made . . . for one night! But he chose Renee Zellweger over Jen. Ouch!

c. *Gerard Butler*: Did they or didn't they? I'll bet

they did. Every photo of them during the summer filming *The Bounty* was of the two of them hugging and holding each other. I think he hit it and quit it! Another bedroom romp? If they did go out, it never left the hotel.

d. *Brad Pitt:* Secretly she still thinks they're going out. She's saved his voice mails for God's sake! And she talks about him nonstop in every interview she does! Give it up! Jen, you have one of the most powerful publicists in Hollywood and you hire the same writers and photographers to write and shoot all of your interviews (your BFF, Kristin Hahn, interviewed you and wrote the 2009 September issue of *Elle* on which you were the cover) and yet it still always paints you as "lonely" and "pathetic" and missing Brad and talking about him!

BLOGG

And the Perezzie for BEST JEN ANISTON BOYFRIEND is:

Bradley Cooper! They went on one date and then he never called her again! First he denied ever even knowing her ("I met her three times in my life."); then he denied dating her; then he denied dating her again (but again where there's smoke, there's fire!). They were finally spotted out having dinner. No matter how many times Jen tells friends that she's dating him, he keeps going on the record (or has his publicist do the dirty work) saying they aren't fucking! Oops. Poor Jen. Again.

They went on one date and then he never called her again!

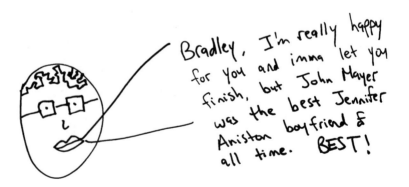

Bradley, I'm really happy for you and imma let you finish, but John Mayer was the best Jennifer Aniston boyfriend of all time. BEST!

★ BEST SECRET SHRINE ★

We spend a lot of our time as "normal" people worshipping the ground that celebrities walk on. But celebrities too have their gods they bow down to. You don't think Rachael Ray bows down to Martha Stewart? But some idol worship isn't as obvious as that. So here are the nominations for BEST SECRET SHRINE:

the nominations:

a. *Miley Cyrus's penis shrine to Justin Gaston:* Gee, I wonder what she saw in this guy. He's the tall, hunky, twenty-year-old underwear model. She's this supposedly pure sixteen-year-old pop-star

They don't call her Slutty Cyrus for nothing!

virgin. Right. Says Billy Ray's pride and joy: "I've never been closer to the Lord since I met him." Do you believe her? Well, she's definitely getting close to something. How many sweet sixteens grind against stripper poles onstage, have nude photo scandals, and date well-hung older underwear models? Exactly. She's definitely doing the nasty and then some! They don't call her Slutty Cyrus for nothing!

b. *Jen Aniston's secret shrine to Brad Pitt:* It's like a high school locker with photos of him from *Thelma & Louise* and *Fight Club*, and then a dartboard consisting of Angelina Jolie's *W* magazine cover where she's breast-feeding one of the twins. She also has a bowl filled with Smart Water that she offers up to the Brad Pitt Shrine Gods every day.

It's like a high school locker with photos of him from *Thelma & Louise* and *Fight Club*, and then a dartboard consisting of Angelina Jolie's *W* magazine cover where she's breast-feeding one of the twins.

c. *Jessica Simpson's Maytag shrine:* It's not really a shrine so much as it is a refrigerator. But it's a great place to go when Jess needs time alone to think. Shelves stocked with Cheez Whiz, pitchers of Kool-Aid, cases of CoolWhip, Chipwiches, CapriSun's, Ding Dongs, Ho-Hos, Twinkies. She doesn't just get mad—she gets hungry!

d. *Heidi Montag's publicity shrine:* In it? All the phone numbers and e-mail addresses for gossip reporters, paparazzi, and magazine editors. Yeah, she goes there when things get too quiet. She'll phone up a couple of photogs and *Us Weekly* and *In Touch* reporters. "Hey, I'm thinking about going shopping on Robertson Boulevard this July Fourth wearing an American flag bikini. In case anyone is interested."

And the winner for
BEST SECRET SHRINE is:

Jennifer Aniston's secret shrine to Brad Pitt. She says she's over him, but in every interview she ever gives, she has to bring him up! Remember how nervous she looked when she appeared on Jimmy Fallon's talk show? She looks like if you just even begin to mention the names Brad or Angelina that she'll jump off a bridge. Three words: Get. Over. It.

★ BEST HAIRPIECE ★

Everyone knows that looking good is the most important part of being famous in Hollywood. Talent comes secondary. Just ask Kristin Cavallari! But if you don't have the perfect look, Hollywood is the perfect place to get it fixed. Whether it's boobs, face, teeth, or even hair—Hollywood's got the right doc or stylist to make it happen. Here are the nominations for the Perezzie for BEST HAIRPIECE:

the nominations:

a. *Jeremy Piven:* His is pretty awful. And I don't understand why this guy even has a hairpiece—he looks like the shaved-head-type guy anyway. If you look at old movies of him before he became Ari Gold on *Entourage*, his line was receding faster than his ex-buddy John Cusack's career.

b. *John Travolta:* He's got one of the best. It looks the most real. But still so fake! We all know it. There was a photo a long time ago, I think, that ran in some tabloid that illustrated very well his hairpiece coming off—it was like this little bandaged adhesive thingy that was peeling off on some hot day. I'd expect a guy like Travolta to have the best; he's worth zillions and needs it to look good when it's flowing in the wind at thirty thousand feet altitude aboard one of his jets.

c. *Brendan Fraser:* He's got something. Dead animal? Whatever it is, he's not half as bald as he used to be. Of course we only see him once every couple of years when a sequel to *The Mummy* comes out.

Bad hair plugs

d. *Jon Gosselin:* Nice hair plugs, but definitely not Hollywood-worthy. He probably got them done in Pennsylvania. Hey—it's an invitation to get them redone! You can't trust any kind of surgery work done outside of Hollywood. Look at Jon's wife, Kate: She got a tummy tuck and the doctor's daughter ended up banging her husband!

He's got something. Dead animal?

And the winner for the BEST HAIRPIECE is:

Matthew McConaughey: He's got the best! I didn't even mention him above because he's in a totally different category from all of the other baldies. I need to find out who

did his and I need to call them! If you look back at 2001 and 2002, he was so bald! He was missing the top of the front of his hair. Now he's got a full, luxurious head of hair. You can't regrow that kind of hair naturally! So whoever did him, I want to find out and go to that person.

And of course in this category, by saying "Best" hairpiece, I really mean worst. But being that this is a book about absurdity, best hairpiece is something to just laugh at. Why not just go bald? So this is a confusing category because in that case, the "winner" for best hairpiece, by default, is Jon Gosselin. He's actually the only one we can prove had anything done, though it's obvious all of the others did.

Prior to the main awards show, many technical awards were given out. Here they are:

★ BEST VOODOO DOLL ★

Jennifer Aniston's "Angelina" voodoo doll. I'm pretty sure she has one, right? I mean, c'mon, you don't think she sits at home and sticks pins into a little doll with big lips and a bunch of kids? I bet she does. She probably has all of the accompanying Shiloh, Maddox, Pax, Zahara, Knox, and Vivienne dolls that go along with it. Damn all those happy kids!

She probably has all of the accompanying Shiloh, Maddox, Pax, Zahara, Knox, and Vivienne dolls that go along with it. Damn all those happy kids!

★ BEST OH, THEY'VE ALREADY ★ SPLIT MOMENT

Mel Gibson and wife had quietly been split for more than two years. Supposedly she stayed with him while he was beating that whole anti-Semitic flap. Who knew? Maybe that's why he's been spotted canoodling all over the world with Russian chanteuse Oksana Grigorieva. Now she's having his baby!

★ BEST ACT OF DOUCHERY ★

You know you're the biggest douche bag of the year when nine months into the year, you eclipse someone who's been a douche for at least nine months more than you—and you do it all in one night! Therefore, no, Jon Gosselin is not the "official" douche of the year. That award goes to Kanye West for charging the stage at the 2009 MTV Video Music Awards.

TWILIGHT:

VAMPIRES THAT DON'T SUCK

Celebrity took a major turn for the better in 2009. Whereas all of the young stars we ever cared about in the past few years were famous because of drug scandals, or nude photo "leaks" and sex tapes, all of a sudden we started caring about an otherwise unknown cast of a vampire movie (two of the stars weren't even twenty-one yet), the salacious focal point of which is celibacy. An article in feminist pop-culture magazine *Bitch* referred to the series as "abstinence porn." But the heavy panting in the movie got so many young'uns all hot and bothered, it's a wonder there wasn't an outbreak of teen pregnancies that year. Oh, wait. There was. And then the screaming began.

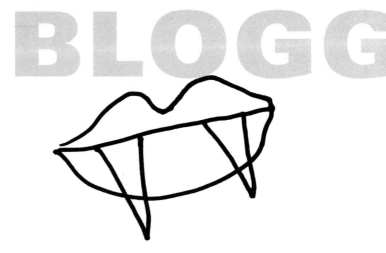

We spent so much time in the gossip world talking about Lindsay Lohan, a twentysomething who hasn't been in a hit movie in more than five years. Or Vanessa Hudgens, who's never carried her own movie, or Paris Hilton, who's NEVER been in a hit movie. Along comes Kristen Stewart (Ahhhhh, I hate you, Kristen! You kissed Rob! No fair!), who not only steals the heart of the hottest thing in Hollywood (Oh, Rooooooobbbbb...I neeeeeeed you to bite me) but then lands roles in *The Runaways* and stars opposite James Gandolfini in *Welcome to the Rileys*. As for Taylor Lautner? (OMG! OMG! OMG! Sign my thong, Taylor! Puhleeeeze!) He's got soccer moms in their forties sweating over him at the tender age of seventeen. Kinda gross, but it's made him a big deal.

"robsten"

A little math equation: Kristen Stewart + Robert Pattinson = Robsten. I think it's real. I do. There have been so many reports on these two. Are they? Aren't they? Dating? Banging? Is he gay? Is she gay? Are they friends? Lovers? Convenient on-set lovers? The answer? I think it's young love. You don't buy a girl a vintage four-hundred-dollar concert T-shirt on eBay just 'cuz she's a good buddy. I don't know how deep it goes. Deeper than their snow-white skin? It's too soon to say, but like any other young couple in love, it's an exploration period. They definitely have a strong friendship—and how many young gorgeous kids are out there as "just friends" together? Not too many.

It's not like she's Sharon Stone who's got 273 notches on her bedposts and he's some George Clooney who had to build a belt rack for all his notches. They are young and getting it on. I don't know how serious it is or how long it will last, but it's definitely on. Anytime they had to spend time apart when not filming, they seemed to be miserable and missing each other. Then they'd run into each other's arms and spend every second together upon being reunited. Or maybe it's all

■ ■ ■ ■ ■ ■ ■ ■ ■ ■ ■ ■ ■

A little math equation: Kristen Stewart + Robert Pattinson = Robsten. I think it's real.

■ ■ ■ ■ ■ ■ ■ ■ ■ ■ ■ ■ ■

STD ALERT.

TWILIGHT
HERPES
OUTBREAK

Ewww!

Don't
Get
infected!

Use
a
condom!

a hoax! The *Twilight* fans are kind of scary and they don't want to believe anything they read—only what they feel.

the taylor effect

It's so creepy how Taylor Lautner's being sexualized. He just turned seventeen and women go crazy for him the second he takes his shirt off! Kind of weird to look at him and say he's hot, because he's so young. It's like because all of a sudden he has muscles, he's a man—and that's not the case. No one ever said they thought Zac Efron was "hot" when he was sixteen. He was just "cute," so this is all going a little overboard. I'm not a creepy perve child molester, but Taylor is hot. I'll go ahead and say it. And he's prob-

ably also thankful he's keeping his job. In many ways he's a better star than Robert Pattinson: He's friendlier and warmer, he doesn't mind talking to media, and, in general, he just smiles more. Very few celebs who fuck over the media and aren't fan-friendly—aka smiling in paparazzi shots—have longevity. You hear that, Russell Crowe and Colin Farrell?

I'm not obsessed with *Twilight*—but I get it. It's the ultimate Hollywood cult film, and they better hurry up and film and release as many as possible before the public loses interest (or Ashley Greene starts to wrinkle). I'm not the obsessive

It's so creepy how Taylor Lautner's being sexualized. He just turned seventeen and women go crazy for him the second he takes his shirt off!

type. I don't get caught up with things of the moment. I think someone like Lady Gaga not Harry Potter or Edward and Bella will actually have longevity. I'm not dissing it. I didn't read the books. I don't have time to read books! (CONFESSION: I don't watch TV and barely read magazines. I go to concerts and watch movies—that's about it.) But I did see *Twilight*. I liked it. I didn't loove it. But I liked it.

■ ■ ■ ■ ■ ■ ■ ■ ■ ■ ■ ■ ■

I'm not obsessed with *Twilight*—but I get it. It's the ultimate Hollywood cult film, and they better hurry up and film and release as many as possible before the public loses interest.

■ ■ ■ ■ ■ ■ ■ ■ ■ ■ ■ ■ ■

I'm not sure what will happen with *Twilight* down the road. The buzz after the first *Twilight* film is certainly as high as it could ever be. I think *New Moon* will probably make even more money and then *Eclipse* will gross even more. How high can it go? And then there are rumors the producers want to branch out and give some of the individual characters their own solo movies. Well, if it gets that far, then we're talking X-Men-type success. I'm not sure if it's got the international appeal for that. I think ultimately *Twilight* will be more like a fortuitous moment in time. Producers are trying to bang out two movies quickly and less than a year apart. That to me is a sign it's all about the money.

2

BEHIND
THE CURTAIN

WHAT THEY SAY VS. WHAT THEY MEAN

SMELL THE BULL SHIZ

Certainly celebrities still haven't learned to shut their mouths. Whether they're talking about their exes, their spouses, their friends, or their enemies, celebrities tend to just let loose. Sometimes they lie, sometimes they twist the truth, but they ALWAYS spill way too much. They love to talk about sex and how amazing it is when they have it. As if regular people couldn't dare have the insane, chandelier-swinging bang-fests that celebrities have. Heidi Montag? She told *Playboy* she has days where she has orgasms twenty to thirty times. But she didn't specify if that was with Spencer's little pecker or whether she did it just looking at her reflection. Celebrities like to talk about kissing, eating, and anything else that is full of emotion. But sometimes they like to skirt around an issue too. Here are some of my favorite lies, critiques, quotes, catty comments, sayings, and amens of the year.

"Certain journalists have written horrible things, and then they've gotten cancer or . . . a tumor, or they've died. It's terrible for them, but they've done really evil things. I truly believe things come back around."
—Heather Mills

I hope they aren't talking about me! At least they called me a journalist.

★

"Don't take a picture of your wife's butt. That's silly. Take pictures of other people's wives' butts."
—Brad Pitt

Hmmm. Looking at other people's butts got you in trouble once before, Brad. Right, Jen?

★

"On the way to the Academy Awards, we started kissing passionately. And, well, let's just say we missed the red carpet and I ended up with almost no makeup on."
—Jada Pinkett Smith

I'm calling bullshit on this one! Sorry, kids! But don't they have a couple of kids and aren't they old and haven't they been together for, like, ever? No way they are that passionate and certainly not

on Oscar night when nerves are running high. Survey says: LIES! PS: Who the hell says that kind of stuff? Have you ever been at dinner or at a party and in conversation with someone where they say things like that? It makes you totally uncomfortable and you can tell immediately there are underlying issues there—otherwise there would be no reason to say stuff like that.

"Tom [Cruise] never . . . said, 'That is what you should be doing,' because he would never do that. He and Katie have their beliefs . . . but Victoria and I have also got our own."
—David Beckham

He may not have said those exact words, but he probably did say something like "Hey, David, ever think about Scientology?" I mean, really, do religion or personal belief systems not come up amongst best friends? That's like me never discussing my sexuality with my best friend. Though I'll bet Tom's never discussed his sexuality with David.

★

"No one knows that woman [Angelina Jolie]. She's a complete ice queen, which is perfect."
—Evangeline Lilly

I would call Nicole Kidman an ice queen. I think Evangeline needs to look up the definition and come back to me after she's read it. But this is a perfect example of what it takes to make it in Hollywood. Evangeline is so minor league compared to Angelina. What Evangeline Lilly is basically saying is she's afraid of a big-time movie star like Angelina Jolie.

★

"My dad won't let me fix my teeth or cut my hair. He loves it! He's like, 'It's you!' "
—Miley Cyrus

What she's really trying to say is that the second she turns eighteen and doesn't need her dad's permission, she's fixing those chompers and getting a boob job! I don't blame her!

★

"I drunk-dialed Jennifer Lopez! It wasn't my finest moment."
—Jen Aniston

Okay, I'm not a shrink, but that revelation TOTALLY means she drunk-dials Brad, right? I mean, she hardly knows Jennifer Lopez, so if she's drunk-dialing her, she HAS to be drunk-dialing her ex-husband! Duh. Think about it: Who do you drunk-dial more—close friends and ex-boyfriends or random people you barely know? Exactly!

★

"I became a star only by association. We would go to the Oscars and I would think, I'm here to support him [Tom Cruise]. I felt it was my job to put on a beautiful dress and be seen and not heard."

—Nicole Kidman

That was your job, Nicole.
Remember the contract you
signed? You had it made! That
role has gotten a lot tougher
now though. When Katie took
over as wife, she had to play
mom in addition to wife!

★

"She [Sheryl Crow] wanted children . . . but I didn't want that at the time. We were up against her biological clock—that pressure is what cracked it."
—Lance Armstrong

Okay, maybe not the best thing to say, but whatever—this is my point: Celebrities say crazy things without thinking. And anyway, this makes sense. He already had three kids; he didn't want any more at the time. But then he went and had one anyway, with a different person, when he was at a different time in his life. He's a dude! Dudes talk. Sometimes they are lacking in a "sensitivity chip," just like Jen Aniston famously said about Brad Pitt.

★

"Who is Miley Cyrus? The one with all the gums? She's got to get a gum transplant!"
—Jamie Foxx

I thought it was funny. Whatever. Jamie's been in this game a lot longer than Miley Cyrus and will probably be around a lot longer. He can say whatever he wants about her.

★

"I've never been taken on a date in my whole life. I have never had a one-night stand. I'm a real relationship person."
                    —Sienna Miller

What she forgot to say is that the relationship needs to be with a married man. And when she does go out with a guy, the guy rarely calls it a "date."

★

"Unless immaculate conception is back in, I'm not pregnant."
                    —Kelly Clarkson

She's not pregnant, just fat! She's denied being gay so many times—but how come we've never seen her with a guy? Does anyone else find that weird? I mean this girl has been in the spotlight for almost a decade—and no real boyfriend? If you think of all of the paparazzi and all of the reporters, and none of them has ever caught Kelly on a date or with a boy? Hmmm. I guess conversely they technically have never caught her with a girl either. Damn that Kelly. She's good at what she does and knows what she's doing.

★

™

Preggers? Nah, Just Fat!

SHE'S NOT PREGNANT, JUST FAT!

"It was very humiliating and very isolating.... But, by the way, if it's not painful [divorcing Ryan Phillippe], maybe it wasn't the right decision to marry to begin with."
  —**Reese Witherspoon**

Neither marriage nor divorce should be painful!

★

"I thought it was interesting that they [Brad and Angelina] sat in the front row [of the Oscars] even though they kind of knew they weren't going to get anything."
  —**Joan Rivers**

You know what's interesting here? People may forget about this, but to me it's one of the most fascinating moments in gossip. Brad and Angelina were sitting in the front row during the 2009 Oscars as Jennifer Aniston got up on the stage right in front of them, just a few feet in front of them (PS: I think this was like the first time they've even ever been in the same room together, let alone this close!). I mean, if you think about the amount of drama that's gone on between those three—magazines have been built around that story line! Did you watch the Oscars this year to see *Slumdog Millionaire* win everything, or did you tune in to catch a glimpse of the look on

Brangelina's face when Jen came out to present an award...and gloat that her movie made more than theirs?

"If it's an amazing movie that I'm really passionate about, and if that's [being willing to strip for her fans] what it calls for, then we'll see."
                    —Vanessa Hudgens

Oh Vanessa, I didn't realize you already filmed a movie called *Naked Cell Phone Photos I'll Take in My Dressing Room and Send to My Boyfriend.* If so, looks like it only got picked up for distribution in Bloggywood.

★

"Commitment is like giving somebody the responsibility of your happiness, like...'You make sure . . . I have somebody to hold on cold winter nights, and . . . if anybody messes with me, you'll beat them up.' Other than that, I don't see the point of marriage."
                    —Michelle Rodriguez

What she's really trying to say? I'm gay!

★

"I'm single again—and I wouldn't have it any other way."
—Guy Ritchie

Preach on, brother! As long as he lasted with Madonna, he probably felt like a prisoner. When you marry Madonna, you marry more than her. You marry her, her fans, her career, Kabbalah, and her weird arms.

★

"This heart didn't come with instructions."
—John Mayer

Sorry, Jen! Some people just know how to use it intuitively, but he's clearly clueless.

★

> "I love Doritos. I'm usually watching *The Biggest Loser*, eating Doritos."
> —Halle Berry

Lies! No way! Halle Berry does not sit in bed and eat Doritos. She's saying she does to sound more normal, but let me tell you what all celebrities do: They eat healthy and organic. Maybe not Gerard Butler and Seth Rogan, but Halle Berry definitely does. If she eats a Dorito, it's one Dorito. Not a bunch. Sorry. Busted. No way. By the way, isn't she diabetic?

> "I think that, at a certain point, doesn't something happen when people just start hating you? I think that's gonna happen."
> —Kate Winslet

I don't think so. People don't hate Meryl Streep. She's been around a lot longer. There's something about Kate that's very likable, very relatable. Don't fuck it up.

BLOGG

"Was I, like, sleepwalking and kissed a girl and there's a picture or something?"
—Kelly Clarkson

There's nothing wrong with being gay. If you are, you should own up to it. What Kelly is really trying to say is, "I dig snatch!"

★

"There are episodes that I watch when I actually annoy myself. I just want to be, like, 'Get it together!'"
—**Lauren Conrad**

Hey, Lauren, I saw that same episode[s]!

★

"I still have cassette tapes of messages from my first boyfriend [and] my husband....It's like saving love letters."
—**Jen Aniston**

Can you say "STALKER!" That's just sad and creepy. Though it's Brad Pitt! I'd save them too. Jen should just date Renee Zellweger and they'll both finally have someone forever.

★

"When I was very little, my idol was Britney Spears. I had just come to California and that's just who I wanted to meet. So I was in a store and she walked in and my jaw just fell to the floor."

—Dakota Fanning

I think maybe this interview got cut off short? Because what I think she said after that was, "I couldn't believe how crazy she was! Shaved head and all!"

★

"We've gone out peed on without people knowing."

—Angelina Jolie

Ewww. Keep the bedroom secrets to yourselves, kids!

★

"I remember Jett when he was born, and I saw him when he was a few months old. It's just horrific."

—Tom Cruise on Jett Travolta's death

What Tom Cruise is really saying here is, "Yeah, sorry. I'm not really friends with the Travoltas anymore. So this is an awkward question for me to answer."

★

"Once I've worn a dress, I can never wear it again."
—Paris Hilton

That's because it's usually stained so much with man juice and vodka and God knows what else, it's unwearable!

CELEBRITIES WHO TIP OFF THE PAPARAZZI

THIS IS HOW IT'S REEEEALLY DONE!

We've touched on this subject before, and I don't want to out tooooo many celebrities here, but do you ever wonder how paparazzi photographers "find" so many of the same celebrities? It's not like the paps have secretly chipped them with GPS.

So, exactly how is it possible that we don't spot Tom Cruise for weeks and weeks, but the second he touches down in Australia to visit Katie Holmes and Suri after having been apart for several weeks (oh, by the way, he's carrying a dozen roses and is perfectly coiffed), photographers are conveniently there to capture it all? They capture the emotional reunion of Suri running into Daddy's arms, Tom and Katie's romantic kiss, the whole family rolling around in the park on the grass. How convenient! Ahhh, the good moments. This happened to a T in August of 2009. Like clockwork. And only one photographer conveniently got the shots—because when someone like Tom Cruise wants to be invisible and not seen, he can. He's got major resources (private jets, money, security, fast cars, top-notch publicity, and management firms) to make that happen. BUT . . . when he wants to be spotted, that's easy too: He's got major resources for that (private jets, money, security, fast cars, top-notch publicity, and management firms). Let's not forget what a PR firm does: PUBLIC RELATIONS. Part of that is image. Guys like Tom Cruise pay big bucks for top-notch PR, and they'll do whatever it takes to get the right image across. It's not different from combing your hair and tucking your shirt in. It's all part of the image.

■ ■ ■ ■ ■ ■ ■ ■ ■ ■ ■ ■ ■ ■

Guys like Tom Cruise pay big bucks for top-notch PR, and they'll do whatever it takes to get the right image across.

■ ■ ■ ■ ■ ■ ■ ■ ■ ■ ■ ■ ■ ■

The real story? Several outlets reported Tom got into a big blowup fight with Katie that week. I guess the roses wilted! Apparently Katie was pissed at Thomas for signing autographs for his fans and posing for pictures just merely minutes after arriving! Katie wanted Tom to pay attention to her and Suri! Can you blame her?

Ever wonder how Tori Spelling's every move is documented? Her vacations, shopping sprees, workouts? She's gotta get money somehow—her show is on the Oxygen network! It's not like she's pulling in millions. She once told *Us Weekly* that she feels pressure to lose weight because the paparazzi are always photographing her. Well, then stop frequenting Cross Creek Park (aka Paparazzi Park), where all the celebs go to get snapped with their kids, Tori.

What about Heidi and Spencer? They like working with the paparazzi and splitting the profits!

There are various reasons for tipping off the paparazzi. Some people, like Heidi and Spencer or AnnAlynn McCord or Audrina Patridge, are shameless and desperate and just want exposure. The more times they set up photo opportunities or tip off the paparazzi, the more shots there will be of them, and then they'll have a better chance of ending up in the magazines and on my Web site. But sometimes this can backfire. In 2009 E! Television's Web site, Eonline.com, banned Heidi Montag and Spencer Pratt from their site. They were sick of the overexposure and feared a constant presence of the desperate duo on their site would drive visitors away. Similarly, the *Daily News* several years back did the same thing with Paris Hilton—vowing to never write about her in gossip columns.

Another reason is money. Paparazzi shots command thousands of dollars and, if done in the right manner, tens of thousands. So it makes sense for no talents like Tara Reid or Kristin Cavallari, who may not be making A-list money, to tip off the paparrazi and then get a nice payday in return (I've seen photogs flat out hand celebs wads of cash on the spot!). It's a good gig if you can get it. I've heard rumors that Jaime Kennedy tips off the paparazzi on girlfriend Jennifer Love Hewitt when he's with her! God knows no one would care about him if he WASN'T with her.

Last, tipping off the paparazzi is also good for damage control. Need to refute rumors of a split? Show your solidar-

ity like Avril Lavigne and Deryck Whibley did every so often when outlets reported they were on the rocks. Unfortunately no one really cares about them that much—so the photos, though snapped by paparazzi, rarely ran—they split anyway.

Likewise, if you're a party girl often snapped stumbling out of clubs, you can always announce your arrival at rehab to the paps. That's the way for a fading star to get her next movie role. Right, Tara?

damage control

So, what's a starlet to do when her nuptials and baby making cease to absorb the public's attention? Here's another perfect example. Let's not forget the night Marc Anthony and Jennifer Lopez stepped out to hot LA restaurant Luau just days after *Us Weekly* put them on the cover saying "THE RING IS OFF!" There were so many rumors that this couple was kaput, the fighting, the career struggles, the new babies. Then, all of a sudden, J.Lo shows up on the red carpet of a movie premiere wearing—shocker—no ring! Just a few days earlier, Marc was photographed out and about in Las Vegas with known Hollywood flirt Eva Longoria sitting on his lap. Trouble on the horizon? Everyone had this couple down and out. But was it all for show? Maybe a quick way to make them relevant again—a transition of J.Lo from being a mom of twins to all of a sudden a sexy, single, sultry vixen? A way to prove her boobies weren't sagging from double the amount of breast-feeding? She's more than a milkmaid! Well, whatever it was, conveniently a few nights later the "happy" couple steps out togeth-

er at Luau and there were at least a dozen photographers. One of the photographers happened to tell me they were tipped off by Jennifer Lopez's team. They had received a call that basically instructed them where to be and what time and what to look for. Sure enough, that photog showed up at Luau and BAM—J.Lo and Marc show up and it's a publicity shitstorm. Now that's Hollywood networking!

surprise?

We see so many shots of groggy celebrities in the airport, you'd think terminals and tarmacs were the only places some of them went outside the studio or Chateau Marmont. But they're not always caught by surprise, like some exotic game in a safari. Remember all of the gorgeous shots of Knox and Vivienne Jolie-Pitt you saw in 2009? No. That's because there weren't any, except of course one public showing in Tokyo very early in the year when Brad, Angelina, and ALL of the kids stepped off a plane showing off their twins to the world. From January 2009 to September of 2009 it was the ONLY public showing of the twins. Brad and Angelina each carrying a baby in a BabyBjörn with the kids' puckering faces

turned directly toward photographers. And every photographer available knew when they were arriving and, again, what to look for. It was one set of controlled photos for the public and that was it. Also conveniently, the photos arrived Tuesday morning, a mere five to six hours AFTER all of the gossip magazines closed their deadline so no one would be able to easily get the photos in the magazines. Since that one shot, no one has seen the twins.

a day in the life of jen aniston circa 2015

I don't get the impression that Jennifer Aniston's life has changed too much over the last half decade. It's like once she got dumped by Brad Pitt, her life turned into a constant scene out of *Groundhog Day* with life repeating itself over and over again. I'm not saying she's got a bad life. I'm just saying I don't see her deviating from her life plans much from week to week. We know she likes to go to Cabo for a vacation after filming a movie. We know her favorite restaurant in LA is Il Sole. We know wherever she goes, she likes to order a Cobb salad or fish. We know she prefers white wine. We know she likes yoga, Smart Water, and Courteney Cox! That's more than most people know about their best friends! Jen is a creature of habit. It's not hard to find out information on someone who does the same things, goes to the same places, on the same schedule, year after year. If you ever wonder if the rumors and reports about Jen Aniston are true or not, just consider how easy it is to find it all out! That said, here's how I think Jen spends her days:

PEREZ HILTON'S TRUE BLOGGYWOOD STORIES

Get up around nine a.m. (sleeping in from all that white wine!), do some yoga on the veranda while sipping a cup of coffee. Meditate, totally washing away bad thoughts and negative vibes (Brad and Angelina, toy shopping!) from the inner self. Breathe. Breathe out any negativity (damn Vince Vaughn and his meddling mother!), exhale. Stretch up, stretch down, twist the spine like a sponge and juice out any stress or drama (why didn't Bradley Cooper call me back?). Shower, put on jeans and a white tank top, grab a bottle of Smart Water, hop in the Range Rover, and head up to the studio for work (must keep filming movies! Two a year! No time for babies!). Stop at a traffic light, look to the left. "Oh, is that John Mayer?" No. Just a look-alike. Keep driving. Get passed by a motorcyle. "Brad Pitt?" No. Just another biker. Work all day. Call Courteney. Voice mail. Call Lisa Kudrow, number disconnected four years ago. "Oh, Matt . . . Matt . . . Matthew Perry, where are you?" Dinner with best friend and publicist, Stephen Huvane, at a high-profile restaurant with tons of paparazzi out front. Drinks with hair guru Chris McMillan. Head home, alone again. Drink white wine on the veranda; pass out alone again.

Any idea what she'll do tomorrow?

THE MICHAEL JACKSON CATASTROPHE

WHAT REALLY HAPPENED

And by catastrophe, I don't mean his death. I mean the aftermath, all of the insanity that ensued after his death. Doctors, former spokespeople, baby daddies, lovers, publicists, chefs, security guards, maids, mediums (WTF?!?!), zookeepers, brothers, sisters, love children, parents, managers, peers, collaborators, producers—anyone who ever took a dump at Neverland came out on Larry King and professed their friendship with Michael Jackson and what an amazing person he was. I mean, how the hell can Miko Brando be a best friend to Michael Jackson and say he didn't have a problem with pills and that he never saw any pills? Everyone else who knew Michael even

R.I.P.

Michael
Jackson

||||||||||||||||||||||||||||||||||||

And by catastrophe, I don't mean his death. I mean the aftermath, all of the insanity that ensued after his death.

||||||||||||||||||||||||||||||||||||

just a little bit says he was on pills and he had a major problem. A lot of Michael's "friends" were just enablers, especially his doctors. But that's the way it always works in Hollywood: You find the right doctor to give you what you want, whether it's drugs or surgery.

First, let's talk about the funeral service at the Staples Center. I think it was important for the kids to be there. But I didn't think they needed to be in the front row for the entire world to see. This was really our first introduction to Michael's kids, and alllll he EVER wanted was for them to be given privacy. Then, the second he dies, his family plops the kids right there in front of all of the cameras, erasing all of Michael's wishes and hard work. Even if they themselves chose to be in the front row (which is highly doubtful), you as an adult or a caretaker tell them what to do in the best interests of their psyches. It was not good for them. Now forever that video clip will epitomize who these kids are. Does Paris really want to be known for that moment in time? It was her most vulnerable moment full of hurt and suffering and THAT'S how we the public meet her for the first time? This girl who walked around with a veil over her head for most of her life? Do we really think she wanted to get up there and say that? I wouldn't have wanted to do that. I'd probably spend the rest of my life regretting it and wishing I could have said something more eloquent. Grieving is not entertainment. But in that morbid year, it was.

There were so many freaks and shady characters involved in Michael's life. I wonder what he could have actually done had he had the right people around him. Instead of booking studio time with top producers who just wanted to make hits, he surrounded himself with creeps looking to take his money. Observe:

★ Debbie Rowe ★

The woman that birthed his "children" doesn't even want anything to do with her own kids!

The woman who birthed his "children" doesn't even want anything to do with her own kids! Isn't that weird for Michael, of all people, to choose a woman to mother his kids who wants nothing to do with them? He's such a huge proponent of making kids happy! Kind of ironic that that's who he chose.

★ Dr. Arnold Klein ★
and Dr. Conrad Murray

This shady doctor and hanger-on bull shiz is the same thing that happened—and under such tragic circumstances—with Anna Nicole Smith. Even several years after her death, there were still news stories and sketchy developments, with random people slithering out of the woodwork. It's the same with MJ. Some of the most famous people in the world get leeched on by douchebags, looking for a little fame and money. It happened to Britney too! Michael was very talented—in the eighties! But all he was known for in the past fifteen years was being a freak show and flawed. Now, this Dr. Conrad Murray, people, before we even prosecute this guy or look into his guilt or innocence, you can just tell he is a sketchy character. You know when you just know something about someone? A Las Vegas cardiologist who invests in energy drinks (a cardiologist who supports hard-core caffeinated drinks?) and who closed his practice to go live with Michael Jackson and be his personal doctor. He's in more debt than Whitney Houston. He should go to jail. You know what though? If he keeps practicing and doesn't lose his license, his business will probably thrive. People will want to go get prescriptions from him! He'll have clients for sure! They'll have a hard time getting pharmacies to fill them scripts from Murray, though.

> **This shady doctor and hanger-on bull shiz is the same thing that happened—and under such tragic circumstances—with Anna Nicole Smith.**

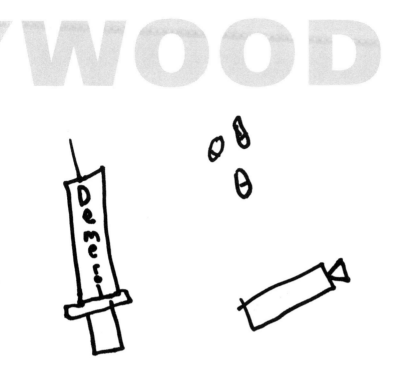

Debbie Rowe is smart. If I didn't care about these kids and did not have to work ever again just by giving birth to a couple of kids, I'd do it too! The best part is she may not even be the egg donor! Who the fuck knows? Seriously. All of these DNA tests, and lies, and drug tests, and physical tests by sketchy doctors—who really knows what to believe? It's all just a bunch of theories! She may just be the carrier! The youngest one has a different mom, probably because Debbie couldn't have kids after her first two with Michael, so he was done with her and her womb factory.

I'm pretty certain Michael is not the baby daddy. I've heard every rumor from a) he couldn't have children to b) he didn't want children. Maybe he could have but chose not to. And I don't blame him. He probably was so disgusted with the way he looked and his actions and mental problems with children that he didn't want to pass that on through his genes. And I don't blame him! Then, of course, there's the high likelihood

BLOGG

I'm pretty certain Michael is not the baby daddy.

that with enough prescription drugs in his bloodstream to fill a Juicy Couture Beach Tote, his guys couldn't swim.

Then of course there are the brothers and sisters.

★ La Toya ★

Michael's sis was rumored to be on *Dancing with the Stars*. You know she wanted it—what else has she ever done? Aside from hanging out on the Psychic Friends Network when she was flat broke. *DWTS* would be the biggest and most legitimate thing she's ever done (besides *Playboy*!).

★ Jermaine and Tito ★

How can anyone possibly take Tito seriously when he says with a straight face that Paris and both Prince Michael I and II are all biologically Michael Jackson's children? Especially Blanket (PMII), the youngest one who has been rumored to be the biological son of McCauley Culkin (suure) and the brother of a Norwegian pop singer, Omer Bhatti, who once lived at Neverland with his mom (Bhatti publically denies he's MJ's son). And having found Allah a few years ago, Jermaine seems sweet, but in a dopey sort of way. They're out there getting paid to go on talk shows, but they didn't hold out for the big bucks like sister La Toya did. The brothers are out there planning concerts and reunions and tours all to make money.

★ Mom and Rebbie ★

Leave it to the matriarchs of the family to keep quiet and stay out of the fray. Rebbie hasn't said anything! She doesn't want to be in the spotlight. She's only interested in the kids.

★ Janet ★

And then there's Michael's talented sister. I'm not going to prejudge her, because who knows what her relationship with Michael was? We certainly never saw the two of them casually hanging out or even saw photos or heard stories of the two of them spending time together. But let's give her the benefit of the doubt and say they were close. Janet showing up to the BET Awards, with her brother having died just two and a half days earlier, was a little bit premature, I think. Giving interviews and speeches, in full hair and makeup. That's a little off. She should have sent a pretaped piece. And did you see the way she latched onto Paris when the poor kid broke down onstage at the Staples Center in front of the entire world? Sorry, Janet, but you weren't even third on Michael's list of caregivers for his children.

The family did NOT need to be there. I understand that they wanted to come out and show their appreciation to the African-American community and thank them for their support in these

> **That [family] is dysfunctional. They all need therapy.**

trying times as well as throughout their entire careers. But PRETAPE IT! That entire clan of Jacksons is dysfunctional. They all need therapy. The chips are stacked against them, with a guy like Joe Jackson having raised them. But if you look at the way Michael's death was handled versus Jett Travolta's, Farrah Fawcett's, Natasha Richardson's, and even Jennifer Hudson's family's—they all went silent. Jennifer Hudson went into hiding for a month and never said more than a few sentences about it. It wasn't until her emotional belting out of the "Star-Spangled Banner" at the Super Bowl that we even heard a peep from her. John Travolta and Kelly Preston issued a few statements here, but even when John had a movie to promote, he didn't even show up for the premiere. Everyone went quiet, because when someone dies, you mourn them and respect them. You don't sell them out with promotional appearances, concerts, ticket sales, tours of their house, and the whoring out of their children.

He did it to himself. Is it a conspiracy that other people gave him drugs? Absolutely. But he asked for them. I always suspected that Michael was on drugs.

He did it to himself. Is it a conspiracy that other people gave him drugs? Absolutely. But he asked for them. I always suspected that Michael was on drugs. And I was so doubtful and suspicious that he passed that physical for his fifty concerts. REALLY? I mean, look at him. He was thinner than Nicole Richie. I couldn't believe it. I imagined he was on drugs and there was no way physically he could do any dancing or anything. That's why conveniently there were cameras there to capture that great rehearsal performance at the Staples Center! So if he passed his physical, what did they test? That he could breathe? Because that's about all he could do. Maybe he gave up drugs for a few days before the physical? I mean, if you consider who his doctors were—Conrad Murray and Arnold Klein—no wonder he was passing tests! It was his own doctors who cleared him. Let the murder investigation begin.

THE NEW SKINNIES

STILL PIN-THIN IN BLOGGYWOOD

In my last book, we gave you some insight into some supposed diets and delicacies of the rich and famous—especially skinnies and fuck-ups like Amy Winehouse and Paris Hilton and Nicole Richie. And while it doesn't seem like Amy has changed her diet much (maybe she's traded the bleach for Windex), a new crop of junkies has emerged from the Hollywood Hills and beyond to give the Parises a run for their money.

taylor momsen

She just turned sixteen but the heroin eyes, black leather, and skin and bones say it all: She's on the Lindsay Lohan

Diet. I've heard stories, she parties hard. Even for a teen. Definitely booze, maybe marijuana. All right, so maybe she's not Lindsay Lohan just yet. But the Taylor Momsen Diet isn't exactly organic strawberries and healthy cereal. It's probably not much food at all, in fact. I'd say it's a little Nirvana music, Courtney Love hair extensions, tap water after a nasty hangover, Courtney Love pubes. Mix it all in with some jealousy, insecurity, and immaturity.

the mischa barton diet

The way to the *Beautiful Life* is to follow the Oprah diet + a little meth. What's the Oprah diet? Well, we know it's to spend all week fasting and eating healthy organic lettuce, then splurging on five hundred Twinkies out of starvation. But the diet that sent her into her meltdown? Drinking a lot of "Coke," watching too much *Weeds*, and eating a lot of pizza with "mushrooms." Mix that in with ingesting some of Lindsay Lohan's fake tanner cream; it's very filling. Then, of course, add in a little Red Bull and cigarettes and a side order of "cankle stew." She loves that. It's a Barfton delicacy her mom makes!

amy winehouse

Well, that hot mess certainly got healthier this past year! Judging by the way her cheeks no longer resemble those of a toothless grandma, she's not living off of a diet of powders and nicotine anymore. Seems like she's back to boozing now.

Before it was just crack. It's all Corona, Red Stripe, Sam Adams for now. Even her family seems relieved when they say she's just into boozing hard-core these days. They must be so proud. Alcoholism is a lot better than being a crack addict. GO, Amy! Of course she needs her protein, and I think she eats baby mice, cat droppings, Pete Doherty's fingernails—you get the gist of it. She's got to get her complete nutrition somehow. Has it helped? Given this newfound "sobriety" (ha!) she probably gained a day or two in her life. She's still alive. Heyyyy!

lindsay lohan

She went from eating meat (and a lot of it) to becoming a vagitarian! She eats carpet, Nair for the hair down there. She also eats crow. Tops it all off with some Adderall sprinkles and Strawberry Quik for the nose, a Lohan favorite.

michael jackson's last meal

His favorite: one drumstick from KFC; he used to love that. He could nibble on the drumstick all week and put it in the fridge till he was done with it. Wash it all down with a pint of Jesus juice. Then for dessert maybe a little pickled corn he thought was a nine-year-old boy's pee pee.

WHEN REALITY BITES

REALITY TV'S BIGGEST BLOODSUCKERS

mcsteamy's naked tape

Technically, you can't call it a sex tape. But you know you've made a damn good tape when it's called a "Sex Tape," even though there is no sex on it. Bravo, Eric Dane! Actually, bravo to all three participants. I mean, anything you get McSteamy to do has big-time production value. There are TV producers who would kill to get Eric Dane in one of their TV shows. He's McSteamy! But to get him on the cheap like the McSteamy Sex Tape, that's a total coup!

Of course, it's too bad his costars were his wife, Rebecca Gay-heart, and a former Teen Queen–cum–reality star by way of *Celebrity Rehab*. Those two sort of gave it this B-list quality about it. Rebecca Gayheart—she made great commercials in

the nineties! I hesitate to call her a fuck-up because, really, she's just a commercial actor. That's like calling the bouncer at your local bar a failure. Maybe that's all she ever wanted to be in life! But her career "speed bumps" (she loves anything with "speed" or "bump" in it!) aside, I think she's stupid. And not for the usual reasons. Stupid, because I can't believe they let someone else videotape them and keep the video. Especially someone as obviously desperate for cash as the sex-addicted Kari Ann Peniche.

And why do celebrities tape themselves? That's like me writing a blog about my blog. Seriously, why do celebrities who spend all day in front of the camera feel the need to go home and tape themselves? Haven't they seen enough of that? I guess when you're at work, you aren't all tweaked out on pills. It's definitely the most viewers Rebecca Gayheart has had for a performance in a long time! I can't even remember the last thing she did. It's the only thing I actually remember her doing other than *90210* in the nineties and Noxzema. I gotta hand it to McSteamy though; he definitely loves her! He's stuck by her all of these years! When you read the truth about the both of them (substance abuse, sex, scandal, baby problems), you would think they'd have dumped each other a long time ago. But they're still together! And he knew her before he was famous, so I definitely feel like they have a real relationship. Meanwhile, Peniche's whoring the story out to gossip shows, denying allegations of running a prostitution ring, and shaking off the whole incident as just a bit of fun—yeah, she won't be around for too much longer. Too bad for her. But the Dane definitely will.

second place is even sweeter

Who can say if Adam Lambert will make it mega-big? One thing's for sure: He's got a better chance than *American Idol* winner Kris Allen. No one expected to lose to the wicked wonder of 2009's singing competition more than sweet and simple Allen. Except maybe Simon Cowell, who was so sure Adam would win, he said so on Oprah.

I don't really care who wins on *Idol*, but it seemed like Adam deserved it. He made Randy say, "You're the bomb, dawg," Kara drop her jaw, Paula stutter, and Simon's nipples protrude with every crystal-shattering falsetto performance. I have no doubt he lost because America wanted a puppy-eyed Christian boy to win over a bona fide Friend of Dorothy in platform boots and heavy eyeliner looking like Elvis in drag with the lungs of Freddie Mercury. Adam seemed genuinely surprised that he didn't win, but he took it all in stride, like he's just kicking a dildo hurled at him off the stage without missing a step. He's obviously a really nice guy. So is Kris. But people actually care about Adam and his image. Kris is just kind of a Plain Jane. Adam is working with really good producers. And he already knows how to entice the media with intrigue.

I don't think Adam remained mum about his sexual orientation because he was trying to keep it on the down low. He just knew it was so much better to make everyone wonder. Even up to the very end. When a reporter asked him if he would be celebrating his near-victory with anyone special, his only response was a sly "Maaaaaybeeeee . . ." Meanwhile, everyone knew that Kris would be celebrating with his new wife, and they were instantly bored.

And when Adam did come out, it wasn't so much this gut-wrenching revelation as it was, "Well, yeah. So?" The gay community embraces him for coming out—and with such insouciance—but it's not like they die over him. He's no Liza Minnelli. I'm sure he could always do musical theater like Constantine Maroulis. I don't think Adam's hot, but I don't think he's ugly—he's got a specific look about him though. He's not my type. Zac Efron,

that's my type, because he seems like a good boy. I don't want to be dating the bad boy, and dating around. It would be nice to date someone you can be interested in and with and not have to worry about the drama! Zac does it for me and for a lot of people. But I digress. Where was I? Kris Allen Who? In the end, Adam got to pose on the cover of *Rolling Stone* with a rubber snake within licking distance of his crotch. Clearly, he's the real winner.

IIIIIIIIIIIIIIIIIIIIIIIIIIIIIIIIIIIIIIIII

Zac Efron, that's my type, because he seems like a good boy.

IIIIIIIIIIIIIIIIIIIIIIIIIIIIIIIIIIIIIIIII

murdered by a millionaire

Next to MJ's untimely death, the creepiest thing to come out of Bloggywood was the news that former swimsuit and/or *Playboy* model, Jasmine Fiore, was found dismembered and stuffed into a suitcase at the bottom of some Dumpster in LA's Buena Park. Her teeth and fingertips gone, coroners had to identify her by the serial number printed on her breast implants. How Bloggywood can you get? It's like a modern-day Black Dahlia murder mystery.

Except this one gets solved. In the search for suspects, it doesn't take long to find out that Fiore was recently divorced from Ryan Jenkins, an allegedly wealthy real-estate entrepreneur who also happened to be a finalist on the VH1 reality show *Megan Wants a Millionaire*.

Instantly, there was an international manhunt for the contestant, who authorities expected would flee to his native Canada. Within days he's found dead of an apparent suicide in a motel room across the border.

It's all pretty grim and sad. But the real screwup here is that the guy had multiple charges of domestic abuse filed against him, and the producers let him compete on a dating show. Megan wants a millionaire. Not a murderer.

really destitute housewives

To be totally frank, I'm not all that interested in the *Real House-wives*. I never talk about them on my site. Rarely at best. I wouldn't consider them real celebrities. They are too old, really; they are the oldest new people to become famous. They're not hot (though some have MILF potential), they aren't smart, they aren't talented, they aren't successful. They are very mediocre. They are overtanned, overboobed, and overdrunk. And yet they're famous! Welcome to the new age of fame.

No one cared about the *Real Housewives of Orange County*, and yet all of these other spin-offs followed. I don't get it. New York, New Jersey, Atlanta . . . and there will be more? I don't understand how they all got famous. I dare anyone to name me three of the housewives of O.C. I couldn't. Really the only housewife who's "famous" is Bethenny Frankel, because she was on another reality show, *The Apprentice*!

They are all looking for fights to get famous and get press; they know what gets ratings. If you sit there quietly, no one will care about you. But if you flip tables, throw shit, call someone a cunt, or just go crazy, you might end up on the cover of *Us Weekly*! The cities and possibilities are endless, I guess. I mean, if you can do a show about housewives of Atlanta and Long Island and New Jersey and New York, then I guess they should do Las Vegas too. If they did, the housewives should all be showgirls and call girls, sort of like all the O.C. housewives are ex-Playmates turned born-again Christians (virgins). All the housewives act like whores, anyway!

Then they could go to Miami, and all of the husbands could be in jail for selling drugs. There could be the husband who's the corrupt politician, and another could be a Latin soap opera star. Maybe they should do one in Alaska; that one would be funny: "We're not all like Sarah Palin!"

But who am I to argue that the Atlanta housewives have got a lot of buzz going? The premiere of the second season was hotly anticipated. What I find so strange about our fascination with the Atlanta housewives is the complete inaccuracy of their titles. They aren't housewives, because none of those skanks own their houses. Ever notice how empty their "homes" are? You'll see them hanging out around the house, and there are no pictures on the walls, no kids' drawings stuck to the fridge, no decorations whatsoever. It's kinda spooky, like they're squatting or something. Nor are they, in a lot of cases, wives. For most of the first season, Kim Zolciak is dating "Big Papa," a married guy everyone says is local real-estate mogul Lee Najjar. In a weird instance of connect the dots, it's also been rumored that Najjar's son is a patron of Brody Jenner's of *The Hills* party scene. And by patron, I mean he pays for everything. Is the reality TV world getting incestuous, or am I just trippin'? Hmmm . . .

Anyway, Kimbo isn't hitched to anyone. Sheree Whitfield, professed Atlanta socialite with some exclusive swamp puddle address, is reveling in her recent divorce. It's so obvious that she's putting on an act like she's never felt more beautiful or empowered since her marriage hit the rocks. Then there's NeNe, who seems like she's happily married, except her bosom buds say she's not legally wed to her squeeze, Gregg Leakes.

The icing on the cake is that, as you might have guessed, none of them own their houses. NeNe, married to an alleged real-estate investor, rents—and got evicted. Sheree's out of dough and selling her place. And Lisa Hartwell, the one with the ex–NFL hubs, filed for bankruptcy a couple of years ago.

So who are these high-drama, margarita-slurping ladies, really? If not house, not wife, what's left? Hos, maybe? The moral of the story goes: You can't put fame on credit. Try, and your ass(ets) will get repossessed.

boyle not burned (yet)

If ever there were proof that ugly people have made it, it's Susan Boyle. The homely, "never been kissed" spinster from the tiny village of Blackburn, Scotland, is not exactly what talent scouts are after. She looked more like a candidate for *Extreme Makeover* or *The Simple Life*. But she had enough vocal talent to qualify for *Britain's Got Talent*.

Maybe the global economic crisis got us all so down, Boyle with her Brillo-pad hair and goofy hip shake lifted our spirits. If Miley Cyrus grew an extra chin or Britney Spears stopped dying her hair blond and started wearing mom jeans, do you think we would still be interested in them? No, they don't have enough talent to sustain them. And, honey, who really does?

Here's the weird part. If Boyle were as young and hot as Selena Gomez, she'd be boring at best. Her vocal talent just isn't that impressive, and she'd just be the new flavor of the week. It's just that no one expected her to be able to do any-thing more creative than belch. When she breezed through "I Dreamed a Dream" from *Les Miz*, she took everyone by surprise. The clip blew up on YouTube and instantly mytholo-gized her. Then she became Susan Boyle, a rare bird in an otherwise same-old, same-old pack of teeny boppers.

Then she turned out to be a bit of a loose cannon. Using the F-word (not once, but twice!) on the paps, the British press, and the fans that mobbed her at a hotel was, again, not what we expected of this quaint, small-town woman. When Brit has a meltdown in public or Avril Lavigne hocks a loogie at another photographer, we enjoy the drama of the diva. But when Boyle does it, we're a little creeped out, like she might really go postal, pull out a machine gun, and smoke the whole lobby or something.

Luckily for her, Boyle hasn't totally lost it yet. The announce-ment of her album on Amazon.com in early September of 2009 brought so many presales, it outpaced Whitney Hous-ton's big comeback album. For now, Boyle is huge. With all the success and attention, maybe she'll finally have her first smooch.

BACK BY POPULAR DEMAND

THE BEST UNCONFIRMED RUMORS I WISH WERE TRUE: BLOWING THE LID OFF HOW IT'S DONE

What you need to understand about rumors, confirmed specifics, and horrible untruths is that they all come from somewhere. They aren't just TOTALLY made up. Some things may sound made up, but they come from somewhere with a bit of truth and get twisted. Rumors can be started by enemies—for instance, you don't think when Nick Lachey and Jessica Simpson split up that their teams just sat quietly and let it all go, do you? NO. That was war. Same as Britney and Kevin. No one has more information about a celebrity than that celebrity's spouse. More times than not, it's the enemy, ex-lover, or ex-employee who's starting all of the nasty gossip. And we the gossipers are happy to listen!

And when you get a situation like the Chris Brown and Rihanna beatdown, where neither side is "officially" talking, the end result is a story full of rumors and untruths. And that's what makes it so fun! Hey, if they actually wanted to comment on the TRUTH and talk about it, then they would! But if they're not, it's going to end up in a free-for-all. With a million Web sites, magazines, and news corporations reporting a million different stories, there's bound to be some liberties taken by someone.

the rihanna and chris beatdown

Rihanna gave Chris an STD—or maybe he gave her the STD. That's been one of the prevailing rumors of this whole chaos. I still think it's no excuse to hit her, regardless of who gave who the itchies. I believe it though. I believe one of them gave the other an STD. I believe she was cheating on him. And I believe he was cheating on her. And it's not like either one of them seems like they are into nice, clean-cut kids either. I mean, they are both getting gun tattoos all over their bodies, and they love staying out and partying till the sun comes up. He's out with some chick

with a mohawk who dresses just like Rihanna. She's been out with several guys since—I mean, is ANYONE hurting from this whole mess? Or were we all just punk'd into caring?

I don't doubt it happened, but is either one of them losing sleep over this? I guess in the end we now know it just didn't seem like a healthy relationship on either end. But I believe he hit her first. I believe they both did drugs, maybe even that night. And look, I'm not saying it's okay to hit anyone, but, if there was drama going down and she hit him first, I can understand why his reaction would be to snap back in some form out of instinct or rage. But he BEAT her. He didn't just snap back. What he did was wrong. Wrong. Wrong. Repeatedly and severely he beat her. And the worst part about it all is that he hired high-powered attorneys and publicists to help manage the situation properly. And fuck them: They did a pretty damn good job. They kept him quiet and out of the press as good as they could. It wasn't perfect; repping a douche like that is a hard job. But they wouldn't let him talk until it pretty much washed over, and even then it was just his little videotaped apology. When he finally appeared on Larry King after his sentencing, looking like a choirboy in a shiny baby blue bow tie, the little he did say was all contrived. Mostly, he just let his mom and lawyer do all the talking. That's the best spin anyone can get paid for.

the pivert really is a pivert!

Screw the mercury poisoning—that was just lame. When Jeremy Piven backed out of starring in a Broadway play

because of "mercury poisoning" but then showed up at awards shows to be seen revealed his true mettle. The best unconfirmed rumor I heard about him (again, unconfirmed—I'm not saying it's true and it's probably not, but . . .) is that Jeremy Piven cries after sex: A girl told me this once, that Jeremy Piven gets very emotional after sex. I guess maybe when someone gets famous, they have a problem connecting to people—and sex, which is the ultimate connection, is a great way to get it! So cry away!

brad and jen's scandalous phone calls!

Do Brad Pitt and Jen Aniston call each other and see each other—Hmmm . . . I don't believe they call or see each other. Nevertheless, so many places like to report on this. Maybe they text. Right? I feel like that's pretty common for exes to do that. "Happy Birthday." "Congratulations." Things like that. Certainly not "Happy Anniversary!"

Here's the deal, and I hate to burst everyone's romantic bubble here, but that moment has passed. It's over. Jennifer Aniston and Brad Pitt don't have much in common anymore or much to talk about. They probably don't even get their highlights done by the same colorist anymore. Sorry. Anyone who says otherwise is lying. But you know what my first thought was when I saw Brad Cooper and Jen Aniston meet up in NYC? Well, there was this report that Jen Aniston was getting out of a limo and the whole time had been talking to someone named "Brad." She was supposed to meet

"Brad" at a bar, and when she got out of the limo, she said, "Okay, Brad, I'm here." This was about a week or two before the whole Bradley Cooper drama began. A lot of news outlets reported that Jen had been talking to Brad Pitt and was going to meet him. Sounds like a limo driver had loose lips! But whatever the limo driver said, I think he got his Brads mixed up! I'll bet Jen really was on the phone with Brad, just Brad Cooper not Brad Pitt!

kelly clarkson is a lesbo

That Kelly Clarkson is a lesbian. I said before I think she's gay, but I have no proof. I don't want to out someone. But if she's gay, she ought to acknowledge it and not hide from it.

dakota fiending!

That Dakota Fanning is addicted to heroin, is a total beast in the sack, and was once a teenage prostitute! Just kidding. But what a great rumor to start! If any of that's true, she'll have a lot to draw from in her performance as the tough teen rocker Cherie Currie in the *Runaways* flick.

hayden panettiere and her tv dad!

On several occasions I've had people tell me that Hayden Panettiere hooks up with Jack Coleman—the guy who plays her

DAD on NBC's *Heroes*. I doubt this is true. But it's out there. Ewwww! There's even a photograph out there that supposedly "proves" it. Double ewww! I've seen the photo; it definitely looks like they are slipping each other the tongue. But he's more than thirty years her senior! And he's married! Makes you wonder if the indestructible cheerleader does have some daddy issues. Her dad and mom were always fighting and her dad has had run-ins with the law. Add that in with the fact that Hayden always dates guys much older (she likes her daddys!). When she was dating British TV presenter Steve Jones, he was thirty-two and she was twenty. Ick. Of course, she dated Milo Ventimiglia, who was thirty when she was eighteen. So see, her dating history certainly doesn't do anything to wash away the Jack Coleman rumors but I doubt it's true anyway!

lady gaga a herm?

Lady Gaga has a peen! I think it's funny; it's a testament to her success that people have to write about her and make stuff up. So there's this video online that went viral that shows Lady Gaga thrusting around onstage, and when you watch it in slow-motion there are like three to four frames where it looks like she's packing salami! I saw the video and asked her what's up! I know she's not a herm but I wanted to know what everyone else wanted to know—WTF? I guess the truth isn't as exciting as the rumors that she's got a peen. She was wearing flesh-colored panties, and it looks like something was there but there wasn't! The panties were all bunched up like a bad frontal wedgie. It looked like there was something there but there wasn't. She just laughed it off. But it would be pretty hot if it were true! There haven't been peen-on-poon rumors like that since Jamie Lee Curtis!

john mayer is a dirrrty, dirrty homo

There're so many sexual rumors about John Mayer. Gay? Straight? Bi? Dirty? Clean? When we were first introduced to John Mayer, probably a decade ago, he seemed like this clean-cut boy who was portrayed as the kid who lived at home and played guitar up in his room and sang songs to a girl he liked taped up on his wall. That's certainly not the John Mayer we've come to know! John Mayer is dirty and he knows it and loves it.

The latest rumor? I heard that when he had sex with Jessica Simpson, he'd watch gay porn. I heard it was true! Of all of the gay rumors about John Mayer, I definitely believe this! I told you in my first book that one late night in NYC when he was wasted with Jessica Simpson, he started kissing me while sitting right next to her! So why wouldn't the gay porn rumor be true?

Speaking of John Mayer rumors, there's also the rumor that after Jen Aniston and John broke up, the only reason she got back together with him was so she could have a friend and

date for Oscar night when she had to get onstage in front of the whole world and present an award in front of Brad and Angelina (in the front row!). Who would want to do that alone? Who would want to walk the red carpet alone on that night? Who would want to walk back to their seat alone? It's a lot easier to have a date. Especially when it's John Mayer and he'll go home and get drunk with you and watch gay porn!

BEYOND
THE CURTAIN

TOP 10 PREDICTIONS

FOR THE NEXT BIG BLOGGYWOOD DRAMAS COMING TO A BLOG NEAR YOU SOON

Similar to Jen Aniston doing the same thing every day, every week, and every month, it's not hard to figure out what's going to happen to celebrities year after year. In fact, it's pretty easy. You can look at a lot of couples and tell which ones will split. You can look at a lot of actors and tell whose careers will fail. And you can tell which ones will get their noses done, which ones will pork out, and which ones will develop an eating disorder. Therefore I give you my list of the top ten things I think will happen VERY SOON:

#10

Adam Lambert's sex-tape scandal reveals he is actually straight.

#9

Jon and Kate will have a spin-off series called *Jon and Kate Need a Date*.

#8

Chris Brown will make a comeback with a Michael Jackson cover album called *Beat It*.

#7

Jessica Simpson will hire the Roadrunner to find the wild coyote that kidnapped her dog.

#6

Heidi and Spencer will disappear. No one will notice.

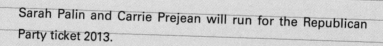

#5

Sarah Palin and Carrie Prejean will run for the Republican Party ticket 2013.

#4

Paula Abdul will win the million-dollar jackpot on *Who Wants to Be a Millionaire*, but her manager will decline the money and say she is owed at least two million.

#3

Paula Abdul's winnings will then be awarded to Ellen.

#2

Kanye West will jump on stage during Taylor Swift's 2010 VMA victory and apologize for jumping onstage during last year's VMA's.

#1

Perez Hilton will read this list on David Letterman's show.

We Know What They'll Be Doing Next Summer

most likely to get caught in the act

▶ **SIMON COWELL AND PAULA ABDUL**

Now that they're no longer working together, they'll probably have to grab it on the go and eventually they'll get sloppy. They've probably been doing it on and off for years in the *American Idol* dressing rooms. Why do you think Simon's nipples are always so hard? He's got a thing for that little nutcracker.

most likely to drop off the radar

▶ **ALYSSA MILANO, NOW THAT SOMEONE HAS FINALLY MARRIED HER.**

most likely to kill a mountain ox

▶ **MEGAN FOX.**

Jennifer's Body famously quipped that Olivia Wilde is so hot, it makes her want to strangle a mountain goat. The crew of *House* got in on the joke when one of them scribbled a mountain goat on Wilde's dressing room mirror bleating, "Olivia, please save me and make out with Megan." With Wilde married, quite literally, to prince charming, and Megan probably faking bisexuality just to get *Maxim* readers all hot and bothered, the chances that those two will actually swap spit is most unlikely. Sorry, shaggy mountain ox. You're a goner.

most likely to get caught cheating

▶ **PETE WENTZ.**

He's already come so close with the strippers at the Fall Out Boy party. It's only a matter of time. Justin Timberlake is a close second on this one.

most likely to trip on the red carpet

▶ **KRISTEN STEWART.**

Like her Bella character, the awkward young starlet is pretty klutzy. She showed up to the VMAs in Converse because she had sprained her ankle earlier and she dropped her popcorn award onstage.

most likely to go to a las vegas nightclub and not get any play

▶ **MICKEY ROURKE.**

Is any explanation really necessary here?

most likely to win an oscar

▶ **LINDSAY LOHAN.**

Because that is the most unlikely thing to happen.

most likely to deny hooking up with miley cyrus

▶ **TAYLOR LAUTNER**

most likely to be revealed as a true vampire

▶ **ADAM LAMBERT.**

Unholy shrieks come out of him every time he bares his tonsils. He must be some kind of demon.

★ THE HOOKUP FORECASTER ★

We've talked a lot about who's splitting up. Here's who we think is most likely to do the nasty before the decade ends:

▶ **SUSAN BOYLE AND DANNY GOKEY**

Their lack of star quality will stop the former reality competitors' careers from taking off, and they'll both cling to each other for comfort.

▶ **LADY GAGA AND ADAM LAMBERT**

Their shared love of wearing gold lamé onstage will bring them together. But their mutual love of peen will eventually draw them apart. They'll stay friends.

▶ **TAYLOR LAUTNER AND TAYLOR SWIFT**

Let's just call them Tay-lor. The boy is already smitten and the girl is on the rebound. So, it's not just because they share the same first name.

▶ **MEGAN FOX AND SAMANTHA RONSON**

The Fox doesn't need a man. She needs SaMan.

▶ HAYDEN PANETTIERE AND HUGH HEFNER

We hear she likes 'em old.

▶ JENNIFER ANISTON AND KEVIN FEDERLINE

Oh come on now, that's just mean! (Then he'll dump her.)

THE FUTURE OF YOUNG HOLLYWOOD

HOW THEIR LITTLE MONSTERS WILL TURN OUT

Hollywood is like China—it's growing by the second. With moms like J.Lo spitting out twins and mom-sters like Nadya Suleman blowing out octuplets, there are more and more babies to love (or despise) in Hollywood than ever before. But it's not always as easy as drunken unprotected sex after a late night partying at a top club (unless you're Jude Law!). Sometimes it's a struggle.

Smell the shiz on this one: Sarah Jessica Parker and Matthew Broderick "gave birth" to twin girls, Marion Loretta Elwell and Tabitha Hodge Broderick. I was surprised. There were all of those reports of "Matty Cakes" cheating, so I thought they'd break up, not have another baby. Of course the news wasn't exactly delivered in the most traditional of ways—or even by a stork, for that matter. *Star* magazine was getting ready to report that SJP had used a surrogate, and their report forced SJP's PR team to put out a press release with all of the details so you the public could hear it from them instead of *Star* magazine. Makes me wonder though—if *Star* hadn't gotten that information first, might SJP have told us anything? Or would she have saved it for a big Barbara Walters special? Who knows what she would have said? After all, I believed the reports that Broderick was cheating. I mean, for a guy who's supposed to be a classically trained actor, he does a horrible job of acting like he's happy in his marriage. At least put up a front or pretend, right? You get paid millions (or, in his case, hundreds of thousands!) to act, so why not try to act happy for a little bit?

So they put in an order for a couple of surrogate babies. I think maybe that was more for her than him. She probably wanted the babies more than he did. So, again, what happened? I'm not satisfied with the information that was out there. I hate when celebrities keep things from us. I get privacy. I do. But sometimes I think there are times when you

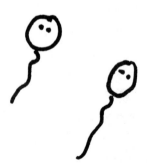

need to reveal some info. I've said this before: If you're going to sell products (perfumes, hair goo, clothes) and charge people twelve dollars to come see your movies and thirty dollars to buy your DVDs, you have to be willing to reveal a little bit of info about your personal life, okay? Maybe not acknowledge that your husband was cheating or that you are having marital problems, but just simple things like the science of it all. Did they use SJP's egg or no? I think they used his sperm.

So after all this—what's gonna happen to their kids? I think they'll end up on a reality TV show about New York City kids. I think they'll be good kids; big brother James Wilkie seems like a good kid and a good big brother.

SJP's kids aren't the only ones who are going to grow up in the spotlight. Here's what the future of Bloggywood has to work with. Check it out!

Kelly Rutherford and Daniel Giersch

BIRTH DATE: June 8, 2009

BABY GIRL NAMED: Helena Grace

Oh, my goodness. Oh to the M to the G. This poor kid. This poor, poor child. They've had a lot of drama. Talk about gossip, girl. I don't think this is the last we've heard of this drama either. I see this guy Daniel Giersch wreaking a lot of havoc upon the GG mom. Poor Kelly Rutherford made the decision to split from this guy while she was three months pregnant with their second child. She said he was k-krazy. That he stalked her, verbally abused her, and was violent and controlling. I'll bet it was more than just verbal, though she's not saying and I think there will be more fighting in court. But I do think eventually she'll end up with full custody of the children as time goes on. She's the full-time caretaker and has a steady job. But I wouldn't be surprised if it ends up violent. He seems like he has violent tendencies. At least baby Helena's got her big brother, Hermes (who shits his pants), to be miserable with. That's right. As if splitting up while pregnant wasn't bad enough, Kelly and Daniel were arguing over how to potty-train the poor kid. Dad was trying to toilet train Hermes and Mom thought it was too much stress! Dad's house you poop in the potty and Mom's house you poop in your pants! The compromise? They agreed to let Hermes wear pull-up diapers until he was ready for pot-ty-training. Better than being an only child with all of this crap going on around you. So what's gonna happen to these kids when it's all said and done and they are older? Hermes will develop potty issues and will only be able to crap at home. Helena will move to Germany to connect with the father she never knew.

Lance Armstrong and Anna Hansen

BIRTH DATE: June 4, 2009

BABY BOY NAMED: Max Armstrong

Lance always said it was the baby thing that got in the way of him having a long-lasting relationship with Sheryl Crow. She wanted a baby and he didn't. So what did he do? He went out and banged his girlfriend and got her pregnant! I guess the Tour de France champ has some super sperm—'cuz we know he wasn't tryiinnngg to have a baby. Or maybe he was trying to prove his peen still had the goods after all that biking.

What's most interesting when things like this happen in "Hollywood" is that we had no idea that Lance was even dating this girl Anna. And when news broke that she was pregnant, a quick Google image search pro-duced nada! This girl was a nobody and there was nothing online about her anywhere. It's like she didn't exist. Lance, a guy who has dated some pretty famous chicks like Sheryl and Kate Hudson, was all of a sudden riding this nobody like a Bianchi. We would have never known if he hadn't knocked her up! But he did. I think they were dating before this happened. There are always rumors lingering that maybe he didn't know her that well. But I think he did. So what's gonna happen to this future cyclist, Max? Well, Lance owns a lot of businesses in Austin, Texas—like a bike shop, a hotel, and a restaurant. So the kid could always manage one of those places if the biking thing doesn't work out. And patrons can come in and say, "Hey, that's Lance Armstrong's kid. The one that didn't make it as a cyclist."

Kimora Lee Simmons and Djimon Hounsou

BIRTH DATE: May 30, 2009

BABY BOY NAMED: Kenzo Lee Hounsou

This kid will be messed up! Because Kimora is a diva like no otha! I think this will be a Rumer Willis situation, because there are so many famous parents. Just like Rumer's got Bruce, Demi, and Ashton, this Kenzo kid has Kimora, Djimon, and let's not forget Russell Simmons being around too. This kid will just be a fuck-up with no restrictions or anything. And he'll want to be famous. But with the Phat Fashion mogul for a mom, that won't be hard to accomplish. So when's the reality show coming? I have a good name for it: *Kimora and Djimon Are Forever.*

BLOGG

Tobey Maguire and Jennifer Meyer

BIRTH DATE: May 9, 2009

BABY BOY NAMED: Otis Tobias Maguire

Yawn. He'll grow up to be boring. Just like the parents. Unless he gets bit by a radioactive spider or becomes involved with SJP's twins.

Trista and Ryan Sutter

BIRTH DATE: April 3, 2009

BABY GIRL NAMED: Blakesley Grace Sutter

Only women of a certain age who read *Us Weekly* care about this family. They don't live in LA, and the only time you'll ever hear from them is when they sell their stories to the tabloids. Their daughter will eventually drop her annoying first name and go by Grace.

Andrew Firestone and Ivana Bozilovic

BIRTH DATE: March 21, 2009

BABY BOY NAMED: Adam Firestone

Another reality star, another whored-out baby to the media for $$$. This kid will appear on the fortieth season of *The Bachelor* with Andrew (he'll be divorced by then), and they will be the first father-son combo ever in the history of that abysmal show.

Carson Daly and Siri Pinter

BIRTH DATE: March 15, 2009

BABY BOY NAMED: Jackson James Daly

Carson Daly's kid will be fat! Just to piss off his dad.

Charlie Sheen and Brooke Mueller

BIRTH DATE: March 14, 2009

BABY BOYS NAMED: Max and Bob Sheen

Well, these poor kids have an uphill battle ahead of them. They're going to grow up and have drug problems, guaranteed. I mean, how can they not? Brooke's had her own problems, obviously. And Charlie's had everything from drug and alcohol problems to dirty-sex problems. He's been labeled a sex addict and drug addict. By whom? Well, none other than his ex-wife, Denise Richards! She claims he liked to surf the Web looking at little girls going down on one another! And that he was so into prostitutes and whores, that he had a madam on speed-dial. See, I'm telling you, Max and Bob have no chance!

Kevin Costner and Christine Baumgartner

BIRTH DATE: February 12, 2009

BABY BOY NAMED: Hayes Logan Costner

Uh, Dances with Stars? What else would you expect?

M.I.A. and Benjamin Bronfman

BIRTH DATE: February 11, 2009

BABY BOY NAMED: Ickhyd Edgar Arular Bronfman

This kid is gonna be a total badass and beat up all of the other Hollywood babies. Beverly Hills High School better watch out! He already made a grand entrance— remember M.I.A.'s ready-to-pop performance at the 2009 Grammys? Her water was about to break onstage. That kid was badass in utero! I think he'll grow up and support those homeless *Slumdog Millionaire* kids. Of course he'll want to change his name at some point. But I advise against it. What's more badass than Ickhyd?

Tiger Woods and Elin Nordegren

BIRTH DATE: February 8, 2009

BABY BOY NAMED: Charlie Axel Woods

The boy will probably become a sports commentator on TV. He'll never be as good a golfer or athlete as his dad, so why even try? Maybe he can be friends with Lance Armstrong's last boy, who won't make it as a cyclist. They can open a bar called Coulda Beens.

Jennifer Garner and Ben Affleck

BIRTH DATE: January 6, 2009

BABY GIRL NAMED: Seraphina Rose Elizabeth Affleck

Seraphina's going to be a good girl. Plain and simple. I think she'll be awesome. She'll probably end up being a schoolteacher. Something really normal. We always see Jen and Ben dropping off Violet at school or taking her to the farmers' market. They seem to be really hands-on parents. And while Violet is always trying to steal the spotlight (she loves posing for the paparazzi!), Seraphina has not been half the camera hog that Violet has been.

SPLIT OR GET MARRIED

WHO WILL MAKE IT, WHO WON'T, AND WHY

Hollywood marriages do not last. They don't. There's always some hotter, younger, cleaner, better-smelling poon or bigger peen that comes along and gets in the way. It happens to the biggest and best stars: Brad Pitt, Jen Aniston, Mel Gibson, Madonna, even Jennifer Love Hewitt, and LeAnn Rimes! Jessica, Nick, Britney, even Jane Kaczmarek and Bradley Whitford! Who would have thought they'd get divorced? Because let's be honest, if you live in Hollywood, the reason is you want to be rich and famous. Happy or not, I don't see Michael Douglas and Catherine Zeta-Jones ever getting divorced—they live in Bermuda! That's how they make it work, by not living in Hollywood. But everyone else can't help but look at themselves in a mirror a hundred times a day. They do more downward dogs on themselves than they go down on their spouses. They spend

more money on boobs and pecs and plastic surgery than they do time with their family. It's a vain town, and looks kill . . . relationships. I just don't have a lot of faith in famous marriages built around fame and fortune in the 90210 ZIP code.

It's also getting harder and harder to step out on your spouse or lover. Nowadays, you get CAUGHT! There are hundreds if not thousands of reporters and paparazzi strolling the streets of Hollywood looking for celebrities getting into trouble. But whether you're Jon Gosselin in Pennsylvania two-timing your wife in a local dive bar, Justin Timberlake flirting with other girls at NYC hot spot AVE, Tony Romo flirting it up in Dallas, or Eddie Cibrian cheating on your wife with a country singer, you will be caught. If you've got a face that's recognized by millions, it's impossible to stay incognito. That's why over the next few years, some of our "favorite" stars have their work cut out for them. That's for sure.

justin and jessica's happily dating status?

They won't get married; they don't seem like the marrying type. Plus, how come this guy never smiles? How do you go from being a little pop-star boy bander with pubes on top of your head who prances around onstage with a bunch of other dudes to being Mr. Serious Artist who never seems happy? Has he forgotten his *Tiger Beat* days? My, how soon they forget! I think JT and Jessica Biel will keep dating for a while and be miserable. I think they have an open relationship anyway, which should totally make them happy and smile! But for some reason it doesn't. There have always been rumors that

WOOD

JT likes to flirt it up when he's out on the town. Hmmmm, we shall see. Only time will tell. What do you think?

Odds of getting married: 10%

Odds of splitting within next two years: 75%

Odds of splitting at some point: 100%

shanna and travis's world war iii—

They're on; then they're off. He almost dies in a fiery plane crash, she rushes to his side, issues a press statement, he tells her to leave and go away, she stalks him, they step out together, they hang with the kids, they're back together, they love each other, they fight, they're on, they're off. I'm afraid for her. Who knows what he's capable of? He shows up unannounced to take the kids. I hope she's got a good bodyguard.

Odds of getting married again: 0%

Odds of getting back together at some point: 100%

Odds of splitting again after getting back together: 100%

heidi and spencer—

They will definitely have a baby; it's good for business! I don't see Heidi's lesser half "Spencing" out on this one—like he did on *I'm a Celebrity...Get Me Out of Here!* and *Jesus.* Two years ago the Heidi and Spencer baby photos probably could have sold for $100K. Now, since the recession, I'd say the Heidi and Spencer baby nets $30K at the most. But hey, there's also the "Yes, I'm Pregnant!" news that will probably get them $10K.

Then there's the baby shower ($5K), the "It's a boy/girl!" news ($5K). Then the actually baby photos, then the "HOW I GOT MY BODY BACK" cover (another $30K). So, all in all, they could probably drag out the pregnancy and birth for anywhere from $80K to $100K. It's worth it! Imagine if they have twins? Double the money! I think they are in love, but they'll divorce at some point. They got married too young and were affected by all of their fame. But ultimately, they are made for each other. I mean, if not each other, then who?

> **Odds they'll split at some point in the next two years: 10%**
>
> **Odds they'll split at some point in the next twenty years: 75%**
>
> **Odds their kids graduate college: 0%**

the couple who works together . . .

PENN BRADLEY AND BLAKE LIVELY—The pressure of working together will get to them eventually. It's like dating your coworker. The novelty of it is awesome at first. You can sneak off into the copy room and Xerox each other's asses (or in this case steal away to each other's trailers to "rehearse" those love scenes over and over), but at some point the couple's on-set paradise will be hit by a tsunami shizstorm. Penn will get jealous that Blake is getting better styling on the show than he is (just because she's the focal point of the show doesn't make it fair, right?). And *Gossip Girl* can't possibly go on forever. How much longer can the voice of Kristen Bell follow the group of overdressed, upper-crust brats around to dish on all their drama? So what happens when the show ends and Penn gets

a role as Jennifer Aniston's younger love interest in a movie filming in LA for four months? And Blake lands a role in a NYC-filmed show? They'll break up, and it will be messy. Leighton, Chace, and Ed will go on TEAM PENN. Michelle Trachtenberg and Jessica Szohr will go on TEAM BLAKE. They'll all reunite ten years later for a VH1 special: *Gossip Girl—A Decade of Drama*.

Odds they marry: 33%

Odds they split at least once before marriage: 75%

Odds they accidentally have a baby out of wedlock: 7%

i now pronounce you mr. and mrs. jake witherspoon

Reese and Jake—They will definitely end in marriage. He will propose and she will accept. In fact, from what I hear, she's the holdup. He's ready to go! He loves her two kids and wants two more! They'll be like the modern-day Brady Bunch. Of course, out of courtesy, ex-hubby Ryan Phillipe will be invited to the wedding, but won't go.

Odds they'll get married: 100%

Odds they'll split after marriage: 5%

Odds they'll have kids together: 100%

lutz and lutz of sex (or lutz new zlut or lutz go to bed)

AnnaLynn McCord and Kellan Lutz—How do I follow up Reese and Jake with these two B-listers? Well, they'll costar in a movie together and have crazy hot sex for months and months. But it'll never last. He'll be too distracted by all the

poon being offered to him, and she'll want bigger peen. But I wouldn't mind seeing the sex tape!

Odds they last: 0%

Odds AnnaLynn has a sex-tape or nude-photo scandal: 75%

Odds Kellan gets with Paris or Lindsay: 85%

jen aniston's shoulda woulda coulda been boyfriend

Renee Zellweger and Bradley Cooper—As soon as they fulfill promotional obligations for their "movie" *Case 39* (when they started dating, the movie still did not have full distribution or a release date), they'll part ways. He's the hottest thing in Hollywood and she's hanging on to her last minutes of relevance. But God bless her for landing the man of the moment! She beat out Jen Aniston in the race for Brad! But I don't see them lasting. I mean, really, Renee Zellweger and Bradley Cooper? No way!

Odds they get married: 5%

Odds they last: 0%

Odds Brad Cooper moves on immediately to someone younger than Renee: 100%

jamie lynn's bundle (of cash)

Jamie Lynn Spears and Casey Aldridge—They'll have another baby and sell the photos again just like Heidi and Spencer. It's rumored they got $1 million the first time around, but I seriously doubt that. So yeah, they'll get married (sell the wedding exclusive!), have more babies (cha-ching!). They'll

make a ton of money and get divorced; there'll be a nasty custody battle and a battle over the money. Britney will move down to Kentwood with her kids and live under one big roof with Jamie Lynn and her kids. I smell a reality show!

Odds Jamie Lynn and Casey marry: 50%

Odds they divorce: 85%

Odds they have two more kids: 25%

busting up

Jessica and her tight jeans: I think they'll SPLIT!

once a *playboy* hussy, always a *playboy* hussy

Kendra Wilkinson and Hank Baskett—She's gonna turn lesbian at some point! She'll get tired of dick, and he'll tire of her. Of course, it doesn't hurt that if the whole football thing doesn't work out, he's got her reality TV show to fall back on. But I don't see the public caring about her very much in another two years. Sure, she'll have the baby and that will make for another fun season of *Kendra*, but then, really, what is there left to do? The whole relationship happened so quickly. It was like a few months after she split with Hugh Hefner, she's already in love and engaged. Of course, I guess she'd fall in love with anyone after dating a ninety-year-old man for that long.

Odds they stay together forever: 10%

Odds he falls for a football groupie on the road: 50%

Odds she ends up on *Dancing with the Stars*, *Celebrity Rehab*, or a dating show: 100%

who?

Lauren Conrad and Kyle Howard—that's who. They're so boring. Does anyone care about them? It would be easier to get Kate Hudson to swear off sex for a month than it would be to find something interesting to say about these two. One day she will realize she has no worth outside of reality TV. She had a bestselling book because she was on a hit reality show! If she wants to keep up the momentum, she needs to be on another show! So I think they will eventually star in their own reality TV show, *LC & Kyle's True Reality*, because Lauren will realize she's nothing without reality TV and he was nothing before her anyway. Kristin Cavallari said she'd never go back to reality TV, but she did! Once a reality star, always a reality star!

> **Odds they get married: 70%**
> **Odds LC goes back to reality TV: 80%**
> **Odds the wedding is filmed for TV: 100%**

mr. and mrs. madonna

Jesus and Madonna—You know she would love to have his children—his beautiful, sexy, dark children. If only she were still breeding. Instead, they'll probably adopt together. He'll leave, and she'll be left holding another kid. He can visit on Sundays. I'm surprised they lasted as long as they did. But every day she gets older. So as long as he can spit, they're fine, because she's certainly not lubricating herself!

> **Odds they marry: 0% (she's not sharing her $$$$ with any more losers!)**

Odds they split in the next year: 75%
Odds he follows her around for years and years and is
in and out of her life like a lapdog: 50%

the most boring
love triangle ever

Eddie Cibrian and LeAnn Rimes—They won't last. It was just
lusty sex. They got each other at the right time. She was half-
way done with her loser marriage, and he was ready for the
spotlight starring in a TV movie with her. It was hot, heavy
motel-mattress pounding. It'll die soon.

Odds they end up together: 5%
Odds they have kids together: 0%
Odds Eddie gets back with his ex, Brandi: 50%

the quarterback and the
supermodel

Tom and Gisele—I think they'll last! She's a "good" Catholic
girl. He's boring and he won't cheat. They'll make a lot more
gorgeous babies and grow old together! He'll retire, they'll
move full-time to Hollywood, and they'll be a glamorous red
carpet couple. Mazel tov!

Odds they stay together for at least twenty years: 90%
Odds they have more than two children: 50%
Odds Tom's ex, Bridget Moynahan, finds a stepdad for
their son, Jet: 65%

4

LIFTING
THE CURTAIN

JON AND KATE PLUS 8

EVERYTHING YOU DIDN'T KNOW YOU WANTED TO KNOW

John & Kate Plus 8 is a lot like the show *Seinfeld*: You want to know more about the supporting characters than you do the stars. You never wanted to see more of Jerry Seinfeld; you wanted to see more of Kramer and George. That's how I feel about Jon and Kate Gosselin. They were the stars but I'm over them. John's "girl" friend, Hailey Glassman, on the other hand—love her. I want to know more about her. I'm not saying I admire her or would want to hang out with her, but she's an absolute hot mess of a train wreck. I've seen what she can do with a bong; imagine what she can do with Jon's schlong. At least I know Hailey's intentions. She wants to party and be famous. You could see it in all of the photos of her acting all ghetto in high school and college, doing drugs, boozing, mug shots—this girl is a class act! Her town of Nyack, New York, was actually so ashamed of her that they tried to ban journalists from talking to the locals. They didn't want anyone coming in and thinking that Hailey is the embodiment of what the town actually was. Did you ever hear friends or neighbors or family from that town talking much to the press? Exactly. No one wanted to feed the monster. They wanted nothing to do with Hailey. You know if I wanted to design things in the right sort of way (i.e., if Hailey hired me as her image consultant to make her even more famous) I would have Jon dump her and then she could go out with Kate Major, Jon's OTHER other girl. Hailey could date Kate. They'd both have Jon in common to talk about. They'd both go lesbian for fame. They don't REALLY have to get it on behind closed doors, like Lindsay and SaMANtha. They could just do very Heidi and Spencer things, like show up at Nobu together holding hands. They could have one too many glasses of sake and end up with a little makeout session after dinner with all of the cameras watching. Then they could French each other and look at the TMZ.com cameras and say, "See, Jon, this is what you're missing."

Now this Kate Major girl—they definitely were not dating. At least not in his head. Did he bang her? Probably! I mean if buying someone coffee at Dunkin' Donuts and sharing a Big Mac for dinner is "dating," then Kate Major is the luckiest gal on the planet! She's found a real winner because apparently that was the extent of their public outings. She says Jon was making her promises they could be together and he'd hire her to be his assistant—he was encouraging her. So her bosses at *Star* magazine encouraged her to leave her job. She left and ended up unemployed when Jon dumped her. Didn't she see what he'd done to his wife and kids? Why would he do anything differently with her?

CONSPIRACY THEORY

Both *John & Kate Plus 8* and *Octomom* were two of the biggest stories this year. Two stories completely removed from Hollywood, and yet found their way into our entertainment stratosphere. I thought it was weird that when the Jon Gosselin "cheating" story broke, there was a crystal-clear shot of Jon and his girl leaving a bar. What was a paparazzo doing in Pennsylvania? Whoever took the shot was obviously tipped off. Something isn't right about that whole situation. How come we never saw him with this girl?

THE UNIVERSITY OF PEREZ

LECTURES FOR THE BLOGGYWOOD MAJOR

Being a celebrity blogger (blogging about celebrity) takes courage, tenacity, cunning, and a certain fierceness. It doesn't come easy and not without a lot of hard work. Are you in? Well, get out those spiral-bound notebooks, bitches. I'm gonna school y'all on the how-tos (and not-tos) of calling the shots and getting the real dirt in Bloggywood.

how to tell if someone is gay, straight, or bi

Sharpening your gay-dar in Bloggywood takes practice and patience. Just because a celeb says he or she isn't, doesn't mean they aren't. So, how do you tell? Please open your textbooks to a little case study known as Licksy and SaMan.

It's actually the question I get asked more than any other question. Is Lindsay Lohan gay? I feel sorry for Samantha Ronson; Lindsay Lohan is not an easy girlfriend to put up with. She loves drama, starts drama, and isn't happy unless drama is involved. Maybe Sam feels the same way? Doubt it. They've broken up and gotten back together too many times for anyone to care anymore though. Despite her claims she hates fame, Sam is infatuated with Lindsay Lohan and her celebrity. She pretends like she hates it but secretly she loves it. Why else would she keep going back to her? It's good for business. And Sam denies using drugs, but it makes me question her sobriety by dating someone like Lindsay. What does Sam do while Lindsay is getting high or drinking? Does Sam just play music from her iPod for her? This year even *Us Weekly* went on the record saying Lindsay abuses Adderall, which she does. So it wouldn't surprise me if Samantha is doing it too. Or does Samantha just sit there and shake her head at her? Doubt it.

Regardless, back to the whole gay/straight/bi thing, I don't think the gay community considers them gay, and Lindsay isn't really into that world anyway. They won't last. They'll probably last a little while, break up, make up, and have crazy, finger-licking makeup sex.

I wouldn't be surprised if Lindsay ends up in jail for physically assaulting Sam first though. It's certainly come close. I know for a fact their relationship has gotten very close to violence. We've seen it before, with Lindsay and her screaming matches. She's always got cuts and bruises on her arms and especially her wrists. Maybe she's bipolar! One minute they hate each other and next they love each other. That is not normal! Unless that's all you've seen growing up. And I can't imagine Lindsay saw anything other than that. And despite being the mess she is, she's still maintained this level of celebrity. Monthly magazines still feature her on the covers as a fashion icon, and directors like Robert Rodriguez still put stock in her. That shows you how big she once was: There is still this residual talent and fame left over from what once was. Why is it still going on? She's the new Tara Reid except she's still famous and gets occasional work. Tara Reid doesn't.

And while we're on the subject, let's not forget the second coming, Lindsay Lohan 2.0: Ali Lohan. The "little sister who could." This girl is destined for hot-mess superstardom. Question #1—did she go to the same plastic surgeon as her mom and sister? Those knockers are huge! And maybe I'm going out on a limb here, but has she had Botox? You're never too young for that when you're a Lohan. And she's destined for rehab too! I don't care how many times they deny anything, their word as a family means nothing to me. I'll just assume they are lying. I mean, Dina has gotten so skinny and I'm pretty sure it's not by diet and exercise. Does she seem like the kind of lady with the motivation to limit herself to water and vegetables while getting up at the crack of dawn to hit the treadmill? No. What a mess. I'm not a prude, but she's a fuck-up in her forties. The dad all of a sudden seems more sane than all of them!

how to become the hottest guy in hollywood

This one's easy, grasshoppers: Have one date with Jen Aniston. That's all it takes. Then there will be a shitstorm that never stops for at least a few years. They'll link you back to Jen Aniston for the rest of your life. But I never saw this coming. Bradley Cooper did it by strategically getting it on with two of the biggest A-list girls (no matter how desperate they may be in their romantic world, they are still RENEE ZELLWEGER and JEN ANISTON). That's how it always happens.

And who would have thought Steve Carell or Robert Pattinson would turn into big stars? Rpatz was in Harry Potter! No one cared. Regular fame never happens overnight. It's a gradual process where you have to put in your time. BUT... big fame happens overnight. It's all about timing. Brad Pitt was big-time but the shitstorm didn't start until his OMG moment when he was spotted on the beaches of Africa with Angelina Jolie.

For Bradley Cooper, having *The Hangover* AND Jen and Renee all within a one-month period, that's how instant fame happens. He was the breakout star of that movie and it was definitely the must-see film of year, so he was going to have his moment anyway. But it would have only been a moment. But he really became the "it" boy by stepping out with Jen Aniston. Of course just a few weeks earlier he was denying even having met Jen Aniston. Then they show up together, and then POOF! Just like that it's over and he's out with old squinty eyes. I guess he's got a thing for older women. And he probably saw what happened to John Mayer and knew things could work out the same for him.

how they keep everyone guessing:
split! big fight! it's over! hanging by a thread!

Keeping the public guessing is a very tricky dance. You really got to know your steps before you try these moves. Brad and Angelina are the biggest targets of anybody in Hollywood, and yet they are probably the most elusive.

This couple fights more than contestants on a VH1 reality show. Or do they? I don't think they get into fights. They make love in the grotto! They make love in lots of places, especially that giant bed they are always talking about where all of their kids pile in together for a big family lovefest. I can tell by their body language that they love each other. And I think they are always together most of the time except in

public when they're not together because of work or travel. But I kind of have this picture in my head that if they're not out doing things, they're at home tending to the fort, wherever that may be.

I guess it's a little weird that we never see their twins, Knox and Vivienne, much but we've seen them a few times in one form or another (being transported off a plane, carried through an airport, sucking on Angelina's teat in a *W* magazine shoot)—I suspect it's hard to bring them with you when you are a nomadic family like the Jolie-Pitts and always on the go.

I think Brad and Angelina are happy, and when they're not, they probably just have Sting and Trudie–like eight-hour sex sessions. That's Angelina's trick to looking forever young! I think they are happy. Together forever? Not forever. But maybe for another ten years. Then he'll likely not find her attractive and want some younger chick. Maybe he'll want to get with Megan Fox. And he can call her "New Angelina." Worldwide this couple is still written about more than anyone else. But in America I feel like the novelty is wearing off. Time for a new kid already! Rpatz and Zac Efron certainly grab more attention here and definitely on the blogosphere.

But what's so great about them still is the idea that you never know where they will be, what they will say. One day you just turn on the TV and Angelina is in Iraq. Then Brad is on Bill Maher's HBO show. Then he's back in Europe promoting *Inglourious Basterds*; then he's in New Orleans helping hurricane victims. Then he's in LA. Then he pops into NYC on his way back to Europe, where, amidst tons of "FIGHTING" and

"SPLIT" rumors, he is reunited with his lovely family, happily ever after. For at least ten more years.

how to come so close and then blow it

Let's be honest, Carrie Prejean didn't become famous until I asked her about same-sex marriage during the 2009 Miss USA pageant. It's funny that the drama I received the most press from was a controversy involving same-sex marriage. Sure she was Miss California but I don't think people outside of her home state really gave a shit about her until that question was asked. So I asked her whether she believed every U.S. state should legalize same-sex marriage. Her answer?

Well, I think it's great that Americans are able to choose one way or the other. We live in a land where you can choose same-sex marriage or opposite marriage. You know what, in my country, in my family, I do believe that marriage should be between a man and a woman, no offense to anybody out there. But that's how I was raised and I believe that it should be between a man and a woman.

So I immediately went to my site and called her a "dumb bitch." Sorry but her answer was horrendous. She was basically saying

that I shouldn't marry whoever I want! Fuck her! I hate her. Whatever. I stand by what I said. And she lost the crown. The only thing she was good at—being a beauty queen—and she couldn't even do that right.

Carrie Prejean is a very lucky girl. Fate brought us together and made her famous. Basically, she's another faux-lebrity who has stumbled upon her fame. I feel like she stumbled upon the answer that she did and I don't even know if she really believes it. But she stuck with it. And has got her own book and career now based on that incident. She became famous for giving a wrong, bad answer. And, frankly, had I not been there to ask the question, and then ridicule her for it, who knows what would have happened?

So what is the answer I wish she had said? I would have been fine with a PC answer; that's what you expect from a beauty queen. She should have said something like "As Miss USA I believe that my personal opinion is my personal opinion and that doesn't matter when it comes to supporting our government." Now that's a PC beauty queen! I don't want someone who is politically offensive yapping their mouth onstage and on TV all year wrong as the acting "beauty queen."

But you can only be famous for saying something stupid like that for so long. Her shelf life won't last. After her book comes out, she'll be over. I don't think she's bright enough to have a career with longevity. She'll end

So I immediately went to my site and called her a "dumb bitch."

up like Tara Reid, doing appearances for $2,000 a night. She'll speak at churches and events, but that will play its course eventually. In ten years, no one is going to care about Prejean. Oh, how I wish 2019 would hurry up and get here!

And it's so funny that this girl got all the way to Miss USA without anyone finding scandalous photos of her—but the second she becomes MORE famous, new scandalous photos of her in bikinis and less get "leaked" to the press. Look at all of the pictures that have come out. Her family has a checkered history—her parents had a nasty divorce; her brother is a big tattooed biker dude—all is not as it always seems. The best part? A few months after the Miss USA's "antigay" marriage comments, it came out that her mom had been in a same-sex relationship.

You know who we should set her up with? Sam Ronson! That ought to fix her! And then she can date Donald Trump. He can dump Melania for her; they'd be a match made in heaven.

END RESULT? I'd still love to take her out to coffee. She won't speak to me. I've tried. I've put it out there that I'd like to meet. But she won't do it. I've repeatedly been asked to be on the same TV news shows with her, but she's refused to be on the same programs. Most producers, if given the choice, always end up putting me on instead! Stupid bitches won't stay relevant for long.

don't ever try to step to a celeb! (unless you want drew barrymore to slur the word "forest" at you)

True cautionary tale. Learn from the master's mistakes.

A while back I was at this Peaches concert in LA. Peaches is like this electro–pop rock–underground cult–type act. I'm backstage in this very small area at the Fonda in LA and a ton of celebrities were there. Drew Barrymore and Christina Aguilera are there. Peaches didn't go on until eleven p.m. It was a long night, and the concert was over at one a.m., and by then everyone was very drunk. Drew was trying to pretend not to see me but I know she did. We were all in this small area, and it was impossible not to notice everyone who was there. While I was talking to Peaches, she grabbed Drew and said, "Hey, Drew, this is Perez." I love Drew. I was a big fan. But she just looks at me all wasted and goes, "You're a dark light and forest." Drew said that to me. I kind of like Drew. I've never written anything mean about her for the most part. There's no reason to. "But that's okay," she said. "I want to be your friend." I said, "I'm not trying to be your friend. I don't need to be your friend." Her gay friend she was with chimes in and says, "Those that can't do, criticize." I said, "You know you're right, but at least I won't tell anyone what a mess she is." And I didn't. Until now. She was fucked-up. She's always fucked-up. People don't realize

that about Drew. Because she doesn't go to heavily publicized clubs or places where tons of other celebrities go. So you rarely see her wasted. But she is. She is not the sober kitten that the main public may think she is.

It seems like I'm always getting in fights just because of the things I say and do, and I'm not trying to be mean. But it's like I'm the only person out there calling out celebrities for their ups and downs. That's my job! Everyone else bows down to them or criticizes them and hides behind their laptop or secured lobby or in a cubicle. I'll say something but then go out there and not hide.

I got in a fight with Christina Aguilera when I told her how excited I was to hear her new album she is working on, because it was being reported she was working with some of the top producers in Hollywood. She said, "I wanna let you into my circle," and I said I'll listen to the new stuff and tell her what I think. Then I said the last album had a lot of filler on it and she lost her shit! She couldn't take constructive criticism from a fan—I love Christina Aguilera! She hated that I called a lot of her stuff "filler." "No, it's not. I would never do that," she said. It was a double CD and it had filler. That's what I stand by. Sorry. Just a critique. But celebrities can't handle that crap. She was really drunk (like sooo many of those Hollywood moms).

After everything that happened with me and John Mayer, I thought we'd have buried the hatchet. But literally just the other day he sent me an e-mail calling me out. Again. I mean, let's not forget there was me making out with him, him admitting to it, him saying these tweets about me where he's offering me some self-defense training (after TEAM WILL.I.AM hit me up), and he sends me this random e-mail that says something like:

"No matter how much I analyze you and break you down, I find myself on your site for hours at a time. I still find myself on there for hours and can't take my eyes off it."

I'm sure most celebrities are always reading my site, looking for themselves, their friends, or their enemies. Anyway, I've come to the conclusion that John Mayer is obsessed with me and has a crush on me. I think he's definitely at least bi. I've heard stories that he used to do it in the back of limos with dudes. He'd have the limo driver drive around the block while he was getting a little man action. Hey, he made out with me, and there's probably a lot of hot guys out there he could get.

Well, that's the kind of trouble you can get yourself into if you try to walk in my boots. Are you game enough?

THE QUESTIONS BARBARA WALTERS WOULD NEVER ASK

GETTING DOWN TO THE NITTY-GRITTY

Back by popular demand! Every week the top journalists on TV from Barbara Walters to Larry King and Diane Sawyer, Matt Lauer, and even Mario Lopez, Billy Bush, and Nancy O'Dell ask the celebrities hundreds of useless softball questions. "How are the kids?" "When are you getting married?" "What's your guilty pleasure?" The fact is, it's rare to get real answers from celebrities. If you fuck them over once, they'll never come back on your show. So no one ever wants to ask the hardball questions. When you're watching these shows and never getting the nitty-gritty, it feels like you're being punk'd.

Here's what we really want Babs and Regis to ask:

Jon Gosselin—How many women did you sleep with prior to Kate Gosselin, and now how many women have you slept with since you left her?

　　—I'll bet he's banged more since he left her!

Britney—Are you currently in therapy?

　　—I think it's really important and she definitely needs to be. Her treatment has got to be ongoing forever.

John Travolta—Why did you finally reveal Jett's autism?

Dr. Conrad Murray—Hindsight being 20/20, do you wish instead of the way you were treating Michael Jackson that you had instead gotten him into a rehab clinic and focused on more natural and homeopathic sleeping practices than the massive amounts of drugs and chemicals that ultimately killed him? Also, can you get me any morphine?

Jen Aniston—So, like, what do you do at night when you go home?

Sarah Jessica Parker—Why haven't you had Botox yet? When are you getting your hands fixed?

Madonna—Do Jesus Luz and you have anything in common? Does he speak English?

Ben Affleck—When did you stop becoming relevant?

Katie Holmes—Why?

Larry Birkhead—C'mon, you're gay, right?

Lindsay—Have you ever been sober for more than three months?

Miley Cyrus—If you could have your virginity back, would you?

Kate Hudson—Who's better in bed: basketball players, baseball players, cyclists, rock stars, actors, or girls?

Amy Winehouse—What's the most whacked-out you've ever been? Oh, and what gets you higher: straight ammonia or bleach? I'm dying to know this stuff!

Rihanna—One question: Who started it?

Hayden Panettiere—What does Paris's pussy taste like?

Seriously, think about it, what questions would YOU like to ask a celebrity?

THINGS THAT MAKE YOU GO "WHAT THE FUCK?"

AKA STUFF I FIND REALLY WEIRD ABOUT HOLLYWOOD

Hollywood is a fickle town. Case in point—Paris Hilton and boy toy Doug Reinhardt. When they split up, they trashed each other. Paris badmouthed him all over town, then ran out to a Hollywood club (photographers in tow) and romanced international soccer phenom Ronaldo for all of the world to see. (Actually, the rest of the world cared but no one in America really gave a shit). Then Doug badmouthed Paris and on and on in typical Paris Hilton trashy format. But then they got back together and Paris started saying things like

"He's the one! I love him!" Okay. See, that's the kind of stuff that makes me think, What the fuck?

A lot of you may remember that I was the "opening act" on Britney Spears's Circus tour. It was hot! On a giant Jumbo-tron-type monitor I introduced her! I pretaped it and dealt a lot with her management, even showed up backstage at one of the concerts. But...I never met her! All of that, and I've yet to meet Britney still to this day. I don't know if she even signed off on having me. I'm not sure how aware she is of anything that's going on in her business life. If she did know things going on, wouldn't she want to meet me? Wouldn't she want to meet anyone that does something creatively for her and then shows up backstage at her concert? I was the taped intro for the world tour of Circus! I plugged that shit to millions of people on my site several times a day! Damn, it was HOT! I didn't get paid anything for it either. I was happy to do it for free because I love Britney and it was great ex-posure and an amazing opportunity for publicity. I never got to meet her, but I guess in the end if that's how she is, who cares? Having done that was even better than meeting her.

By the way, did you know all of her concerts here were rated PG? You know they didn't even allow booze backstage at her concerts? How lame is that? So in NY and LA, when they were having all the celebrities come, you couldn't get booze any-where. Candies was one of the tour sponsors, and they had VIP rooms with no booze and lots of soft drinks. Lots of ce-lebs were not happy about that. Celebs LOVE to drink. And do drugs. And this was a completely sober backstage to protect Britney from being tempted. I'm not a big boozer, but it would be nice to have a drink. I thought it was interesting nonetheless that there was that much of a shield around her.

kate hudson, party-momimal

Cisco's

How does Kate Hudson get up and change diapers and feed her baby a bottle in the morning? You ever had that feeling where you had five too many vodka and Red Bulls—the sugar and the alcohol mixing together in your body all night and you wake up with a headache the size of Cisco's balls? Kate Hudson has a lot of those nights, I think. Luckily for her, Ryder is probably all grown-up and probably makes his own breakfast and packs his own bag for school. But who makes him dinner? Kate Hudson definitely likes to party. All these moms in Hollywood these days, just like to ppppartttyyy. It's crazy. How often do the rest of America's moms go out to big nightclubs or run around the world with athletes and movie stars? I think a night out at Applebee's qualifies as a big night out for most moms! I don't know too many moms who do very un-motherly-like things. But

IIIIIIIIIIIIIIIIIIIIIIIIIIIIIIIIIIIIIIIIIIIIIIIIIIIIIIIIIIIIII

You ever had that feeling where you had five too many vodka and Red Bulls—the sugar and the alcohol mixing together in your body all night and you wake up with a headache the size of Cisco's balls?

IIIIIIIIIIIIIIIIIIIIIIIIIIIIIIIIIIIIIIIIIIIIIIIIIIIIIIIIIIIIII

in Hollywood it seems like the Ashlee Simpsons and Kate Hudsons and Christina Aguileras of the world party pretty hard comparatively. They're probably all pretty good moms; we all see those convenient shots of them sitting in the park playing with their kids: all perfect, no diaper bags around, no grass stains, no nanny. Just a young starlet mom who was out partying till four a.m. hanging with her kid on an easy, breezy day in Hollywood!

the b-list tom and gisele

A-Rod and Madonna: I don't even know if they were ever really together. They both have the same manager, Guy Oseary. All we know is it was rumored they were seeing each other. She'd show up at some Yankees games; he'd show up in her NYC neighborhood. Her kids would be seen wearing Yankees hats and jerseys; he'd be spotted at Kabbalah services. It was allllll verryy convenient. But they never talked about it to the press and no really good photo of the two of them hanging out ever really existed. He's a pretty hot dude for her. And she's pretty famous for him. So they both benefited from the thought of being together. His marriage was on the way out, and what did he have to lose? But again, there were never any REAL photos of them together since the rumors of the hookup, and then all there was were these conveniently staged photos of a tall guy wearing a Yankees hat and workout gear getting off her private jet. But the photos were so blurry from being taken so many hundreds of yards away that you couldn't tell whether it was him or not. That was the intention, by the way! Then she starts dressing her kids in Yankee outfits, just to make her ex-hubby Guy Ritchie jealous. Of course, in the end, I don't think Guy really gave a shit; he was just happy to be rid of Madonna! But the next thing you know, it's over between A-Rod and Madonna and she's on to boy toy Jesus Luz, and like clockwork she has Jesus Luz wearing Yankee hats. WHAT THE FUCK IS GOING ON? In the end all that one can say is that it's weird that Jesus is closer in age to Madonna's daughter, Lourdes, than he is to Madonna herself. That's creepy. Granted, Madge is probably just fucking him and it won't last forever, but it's still creepy. Whatever keeps her happy. After all, she is Madonna.

brad pitt gave up pot? wrong.

When Brad Pitt was doing his press tour for *Inglourious Basterds* he told HBO talk show host Bill Maher that he hasn't smoked a doobie in the longest time now that he's got kids. Everyone knows Brad is a huge pothead! Brad Pitt still smokes pot. Even his director Quentin Tarantino said that during their production, sometimes they'd kick back and light one up. Oops! Brad caught in a lie. I wonder if Angelina does it. Right? I mean, does she just walk by and get secondhand or does she actually sit down and pack a bowl? Certainly not while breast-feeding! And do they smoke in the house while the kids are there? What about the little twins! How does Brad Pitt obtain marijuana by the way? I'm curious. Does he have a producer buy it for him? I'd be so paranoid if I were him.

PEREZ ON PEREZ

TAKING A PEEK UNDER MY OWN HOOD

In which Perez Hilton interviews Mario Lavandeira and gets the true story on the Queen of Bloggywood:

What do you see as the evolution of gossip, i.e., where's it going?

I don't see gossip going anywhere. It just grows and grows every day, like Jessica Simpson's waistline. The numbers of online viewers looking for information is astounding. But there are a lot of copycat sites out there right now. It's possible to make noise if you have a corporate entity backing you. That's what's going on these days; most sites are "launching" with millions of dollars and dozens of staffers behind them. But all of

the money in the world won't help if you can't produce the right creative content. That's why I think there's no site quite like mine. So I started CocoPerez.com to do the same thing in the fashion and style world. It's doing better than expected. Feedback is amazing. I think eventually some of these entertainment Web sites will have to go away. They can't all survive. Some of my so-called "competitors" had good years. Major traffic increases occur during mega-events. But without those events, the average sites are flat. There are a lot of sites out there that are trying to do what I do, and they have forty-plus people. It's insane. They've got to be losing money or at best breaking even. They have too many people working for them, and they pay for stories, and pay for freelancers and video. My book editor wanted me to name all of my "competitors" (I don't really view them as competitors, but I guess we're all in the same online genre) and compliment or slag them off. But I don't want to give anyone any press. That's not my job.

Who will be the biggest star of 2011?

Look at Lady Gaga. No one even knew who she was last year and now she's huge. But if I had to predict the biggest star for 2011, I'd say it's going to be Robert Pattinson. Robert Pattinson still has a bunch more *Twilight* films to make. Think about how big he is right now, and multiply that by three or four. He's going to just keep getting bigger. Zac Efron could have challenged him, but I don't see him making the megablockbuster

international hits that will propel him to that. Especially since he backed out of *Footloose*!

Do you think Jen Aniston will have a biological kid?

It's almost too late now. She's getting really old. I don't think so. I think she came from a dysfunctional family, and she's got family issues and doesn't want to have her own. I mean, she can have anything she wants (except Brad Pitt!), so why wouldn't she have a kid yet unless she actually wanted one?

Will you ever sell your site and for how much?

I would sell half of my site for $500 million. I would maintain 51% ownership and do whatever I want with it.

Do you wish for a vacation?

Definitely. I almost did it this year. I went to Tokyo and worked less than normal and averaged less than six hours of work per day. It would be nice to not have to work, especially since I have help now. I'm open about it: I have help. I needed it! Recently, in the last year, I have gotten help. But it would be hard to take off a week. I don't know if I could do that. I don't really want to do that until my child is born. I'd like to have kids by the age of thirty-four or thirty-five. I'm thirty-one now.

PS: My child plans—I'd like to have five ideally, but after I have two or three, I may realize five might be too much.

I'd like some or all to be biological children, though I might adopt as well. I don't really mind adoption, but I don't think there is anything wrong with the fact that my preference is to have my own biological children. And I'll raise them with my two partners: my mom and my sister, oh and my dog. But I definitely want to have kids.

What else would you like to do?

I definitely want a TV vehicle for me. I was mostly happy with my VH1 show, but they were just specials and aired whenever. There's value to having a show daily or weekly. Just like my Web site is a must-read appointment, I'd like my show to be a must-see appointment. I'd like a Chelsea Handler–type show. I've been taking meetings but nothing has happened yet. I've always got twenty things up in the air, and I hope that three will happen.

Anything that totally bombed that you regret doing?

No. I don't regret doing anything. Sometimes I was advised not to do this or not to do that, but some of those things ended up being the best. Sometimes the silly things, like being a judge on Miss USA—a silly beauty pageant—can be huge. And random! So I never immediately turn things down because you never know what will or won't be fun or useful. Did Paula or Simon or Randy really think *American Idol* would turn into what it became? It used to just be this little show on FOX.

How much do you sleep per night?

Now I get five and a half to six hours per night. I pushed the time I wake up to four forty-five a.m. I sleep an extra forty minutes now. Now I get to bed around eleven p.m.

How many e-mails are in your in-box when you wake up?

Several thousand. Every morning. I usually look in the subject line and read the most important ones and try to delete the rest. Sometimes I miss huge exclusives because there were too many e-mails to go through and I'll glance over important ones accidentally.

Do you miss Bea Arthur?

I do. I was so sad when she died—I loved her. She's a legend. She's a Golden Girl. I met Betty and Rue recently, but the others had died sadly before I could.

BlackBerry to BlackBerry
with Kim Kardashian*

When was the last time you ate at McDonald's and what did you eat?

I ate McDonald's about a month & a half ago in Africa. I ate about a dozen apple pies. I also had chicken fingers dipped in honey!

What was the last book you read and give me a summary?

I read *The Purpose Driven Life*. It's a really spiritual book that helps inspire me.

Do you wish they had just made a movie of it first so you didn't have to read the book?

No, I don't think inspirational books turn out the same on film.

Did you graduate college?

No. I went four years and should have finished with all the credits I have but chose to work for my father instead.

Have you ever pictured the president naked?

No, but Obama is pretty sexy.

Do you download your own music or does someone else do it for you?

I download all the music I love on iTunes! I love making mixes and playlists!

Do you ever book your own travel arrangements online?

Expedia.COOOOOOOM. I book my own travel almost all the time.

What was the last Tara Reid movie you saw?

American Pie

STOP THE PRESS!

this just in, bitches:

Things in the celebrity world happen at an accelerated pace. You don't just take one shot of tequila, you guzzle half the bar. You don't just go to the gym, you enroll in a six-week crash diet and exercise. The same can be said for the rate at which news in the celebrity world develops. Just as I handed in this book, several events took place that would not only alter Hollywood for the present time, but also transcend the entertainment world and go into the mainstream news genre.

Hollywood is a lot like a gated community in that there are several different types of people all living with one communal space. And within that you've got drugs, beatings, infidelity and deaths. Just after I handed in my first draft of this book, we were shocked with the sudden and tragic death of DJ AM. The thing that I found most special about DJ AM was his normalcy. He was a normal human, not necessarily a celebrity. BUT...he became one. The more popular he became, the more famous he became. All of a sudden he went from this guy who just wanted to play his music, to a guy known for dating Nicole Richie, Mandy Moore, and model Hayley Wood. He was making upward of $15K per gig, which by the way is a SHITLOAD of money. He was working harder than most celebrities, flying around the country playing gigs one night in Columbus, Ohio, and the next night Orlando, Florida. Every night he didn't work, it was another $15K he wasn't making. He was one of the hardest-working people in showbiz. For that, he wasn't a celebrity. He was blue collar, putting in his hours every night of every week. And yet, for as much as he wasn't "celebrity" or "Hollywood," there he was out till three a.m., doing drugs, in AA, a graduate of rehab, dating wafer-thin celebrities and models, posing with actors and actresses, calling LA and NYC home, visiting Vegas and Miami more than 99% of the population. He ended up being in the celebrity machine, moreover a part of it. He met his demise in the form of drugs and pills. Locking himself in his apartment, telling the doorman not to let his friends up to see him because he would be sleeping and resting. It's all very rock 'n' roll and Hollywood. But to me this was a perfect example of someone not necessarily cut out of the Hollywood mold, but who broke through and then was eaten up, churned out, spit out, and done all in a very short amount of time.

Then his funeral is attended by VERY close friends like Travis Barker and Scott Caan. The memorial service turns out the Lindsay Lohans and John Mayers of the world, i.e., his acquaintances. It's his week. But he's not a famous actor, so he probably won't be honored by the Emmys or Oscars during their memorial tributes. The MTV VMAs and Grammys— sure. It was definitely his week in Hollywood when he died. He'll be remembered again and will be credited with forever changing the celebrity DJ world. But his memory unfortunately will always be tainted with the way he went out.

So there's your "death" and "drugs" and "overdosing" all in one.

Of course Nicole Richie just gave birth to Baby Sparrow. That's your "birth." And then, of course, a few pregnancies we're waiting on are Halle Berry and Rebecca Gayheart, rumored to be expecting. They have neither issued confirmations or denials. Same goes with Penelope Cruz. The day I handed this manuscript in, all three will probably confirm their pregnancies. But it's all part of the cycle in this gated community.

And while DJ AM and Nicole Richie represent the death and life within Hollywood, we had another beating—this time a reality star and a football player. Beatings don't usually happen within gated communities, a place that's supposed to celebrate safety and security. But when they do, the effect is often magnified because it's suuuchhhh a surprise. So here we were with reality slut Tila Tequila and footballer Shawne Merriman.

Tila accused San Diego Chargers linebacker Shawne Merriman of choking her, one early Sunday morning in September. But then I guess it wasn't so quiet, since police were called to Merriman's house in Poway, California, a small town near San Diego. Tila—who by the way only added "Tequila" to sound a little bit more flashy and gain more attention (her real name is Tila Nguyen)—claimed she was choked and restrained by the linebacker. So she made a citizen's arrest and called the cops!

Merriman was charged with battery and false imprisonment, and the cops hauled him away into custody. Then "Tequila" is

taken to the hospital. While I don't take this situation lightly, I'm sure Tila the fame whore will find some way to capitalize on this with a big interview. I bet she tries to go for a magazine cover "tell-all," but I know no one would actually give her that!

Oh, but wait! Actually, Merriman has a side of his own. It seems like Tila may have called the cops on someone who was actually trying to help her? This is where it gets juicy. Merriman issued this statement a day later:

> On September 6, 2009, the San Diego Sheriffs Department responded to a citizen's complaint that was initiated by Tila Nguyen (aka Tila Tequila). I was taken into custody based upon that complaint. At the time, I was concerned about her welfare, given the intoxicated state she appeared to be in, and I encouraged her to stay until safe transportation could be provided. We would all do our best to help a friend if we considered their actions to be detrimental to their personal safety. I in no way caused any harm to Ms. Nguyen; however, paramedics were called and she was examined but no injuries were reported. She was released and has since returned to Los Angeles, California. There have been no charges filed against me. I want to thank the San Diego Sheriff's Department for their professionalism. I will continue to cooperate fully with the Department and I look forward to clearing my name regarding these false allegations. I want to

put this behind me so I can continue to focus on
a successful season for the San Diego Chargers.

I wonder if the truth will ever come out? Who do you believe?

So there's your "beating."

Nick and Vanessa got back together. Paris Hilton and Doug
Reinhardt got back together. Mark my words, they will both
SPLIT! again. But I'm sure there was some infidelity or fish-
ing in the pond during the split at some point with these
couples. And there's your "cheating."

Just one week in the life of the gated community of Hollywood. Beatings, cheatings, and overdosing. I wonder what
next week will bring us.

ACKNOWLEDGMENTS

Thank you to Carrie Prejean, will.i.am, Demi Moore, Lily Allen, Ashlee Simpson, Twitter, and Jesus.